M.

Ancient and Modern

To: Rev Dianne
my teacher, mentor
& friend

[signature]

MYSTERIES
Ancient and Modern

SAI GRAFIO

New Dawn

NEW DAWN
a division of Sterling Publishers (P) Ltd.
L-10, Green Park Extension, New Delhi-110016.
Ph.: 6191784/5, 6191023 Fax: 91-11-6190028
E-mail: ghai@nde.vsnl.net.in

Mysteries: Ancient & Modern
©1997, Sai Grafio
ISBN 81 207 2004 0
Reprint 1999

Published by Sterling Publishers Pvt. Ltd., New Delhi-110016.
Lasertypeset by Vikas Compographics, New Delhi-110029.
Printed at Ram Printograph, New Delhi-110051.
Cover design by Rattan Razdan

FOREWORD

Many readers of *Mysteries: Ancient and Modern* will have read one or several of the dozen published books of my own, like *The White Brotherhood, The Science of White Magic,* and foremost—my longtime bestseller, soon to be published in five languages, *Finding Your Soul Mate.*

You then know, like Sai Grafio, I too have been a longtime seeker of anciently known spiritual truth! I have personally met and become friends with countless authors and high souls who have learned and lived these sacred truths divulged so clearly and eloquently in this book. Our grand home in the sky, we call Earth, is gradually awakening to the longed for GOLDEN AGE foretold by prophets and seers for ages. This sweet and electrifying birth of golden enlightenment is due to past and present avatars, masters, adepts, initiates, and genuine seekers and presenters of ancient and modern truths, like my extraordinary friend, Sai Grafio.

It has been my good fortune to know Sai—as a close personal friend—for over 25 years. He has constantly and relentlessly sought out truth from the nearest and farthest sources of spiritual knowledge—including our own present day avatar, Sai Baba, in India. This book is a gold-mine!

Those of us who know and love Sai Grafio, look upon him as a living, breathing, caring and quickly sharing "encyclopaedia of knowledge". This book will thrill and fill you with almost whatever spiritual knowledge you seek. Enjoy!

Dr. Russ Michael

PREFACE

Nature does not reveal her secrets very easily. There is a veil that is dropped between spirit and matter which even the most ardent scrutiny cannot penetrate. There are more questions than there are answers, and certitude often varies from one authority to another. The ancients have mapped the highways of religion, science and philosophy, yet modern man must somehow integrate ancient text into modern life. Even after profound revelation, it is often difficult to transmit the gnosis to others in a comprehensible way. The inscrutable Chinese sage, Lao Tse, would say, "Whoever knows does not say or whoever says does not know." In Taoism, the Tao that can be explained is not the Tao.

Truth is one and indivisible from the Absolute point of view, yet polemic arguments continue among the disciplines and interdisciplines who claim their respective verities as tne "absolute truth". Mysteries abide to this day as to the reality of life and death, God, eternity, etc. Love itself is a profound mystery which is rarely, if at all, understood. If we understood, all questions would cease and there would be total rest, peace and at-one-ment with all that is. Revelation takes place in increments and there is a "ring-pass-not" to the uninitiated. The full glare of God-realisation or cosmic consciousness is too much for the neophyte and would shatter his form if revelation took place too suddenly. Arjuna asked Krishna to reveal to him the avatar's true form, the *Vishwarupa*, and had to beg Krishna to withdraw the vision when his request was granted. It was too much for his mortal eyes.

Logic, mental probing, ratiocination and myriads of mind styles do not explain the ultimate mysteries. As soon as one horizon is reached, another one looms up ahead. It would take more than one lifetime just to absorb all the empirical knowledge of just one discipline, imagine how long it takes to approach the Absolute. Plotinus, a Neoplatonist, said that there is this force in the universe and there is no limit as to how far one can evolve into this unitary force called God.

We have gone from the high ethical and moral guideposts of Plato to the ignoble situational ethics of modern day Humanists. Culture and civilisations have their cycles as do spiritual and moral values. This *Kali Yuga* in which we find ourselves contains only 25 per cent light and 75 per cent darkness. We are reminded in the *Bhagavad Gita* that whenever darkness threatens to overtake the world, the Lord Himself takes human birth in order to save the *dharma*, protect the virtuous and punish the evildoers. Sai Baba, the present day avatar, says that such was the case during the Krishna and Rama periods; however, if the avatar had to uproot today no one would survive. The Sai Avatar has come to correct the *Buddhi* or the intelligence of man. The ego has to be destroyed and replaced with a transcendental reality. In other words, God is not finished with us yet. Paul, in Christianity, tells us similarly that we have to be transformed by the renewing of our mind. "Mind is the builder," according to Edgar Cayce.

In the *Sathya Yuga*, all is known and there are no mysteries or hidden things remaining in the dark. *Sathya* means truth and that is Sai Baba's first name. How do we qualify for the truth? Our real nature is *Sat-Chit-Ananda* or existence, consciousness and bliss. We have forgotten who we are and are mired over by *avidya* or ignorance. There is a law of invocation. "Knock and the door will open, seek and ye shall find." The Lord is a prisoner in the devotee's heart and remains there as the *Sat Purush*, the indweller. Mysteries—past, present and future—can be known by knowledge of

one's Self or *Atma*. *Atma Vidya* or knowledge of one's Self
is *Brahma Vidya* or knowledge of God.

> *A little learning is a dangerous thing;*
> *Drink deep, or taste not the Pierian spring.*
> *There shallow draughts intoxicate the brain,*
> *And drinking largely sobers us again.*
> **Alexander Pope**

There is much knowledge today, yet little wisdom. We
possess cursory knowledge of the empirical world and do not
dive deep for the spiritual waters of truth. Sathya Sai Baba
talks about spiritual pearls. It is not enough to say that the
spiritual pearls do not exist and all stories of them remain
untrue when one is not willing to dive deep enough to find
them. We only see one-millionth of the electromagnetic
spectrum and audibly hear only a short range of frequencies.
How then are we to understand spirit when it is beyond the
realm and dimension of the senses?

No scientist in the empirical realm has ever discovered the
kundalini. The *Brahman Randhra* or crown chakra has
never been photographed. The thief only sees the empty
pockets of the saint and not the nimbus or halo surrounding
his head. The consciousness of an individual can only
perceive what the mind of that person will allow; that is, his
own reflection.

We are moving into a new dispensation where thought
and feeling will have greater manifestation than before.
Thought, will and feeling will have to be united. A house
divided cannot stand. The mysteries of life are going to be
revealed and truth will become more evident. No longer will
we be able to be double-minded or duplicitous in our
intentions. The higher electrical currents of the ethers are
merging with the dense molecular.

In past dispensations, only the select few were initiated
into the mysteries. Now is the time when each soul will

become its own magician or priest for good or ill. With the ingress of the seventh ray (Aquarius) pouring into the solar system, truth will be given more definition. Darkness will be exposed as the intensity of the light increases.

The end of a 26,000-year cycle is coming to a close and there will be a harvest. May the mysteries be revealed to you in this lifetime so that you will graduate into the new heaven and new earth. Man can be an acronym for *Mysterion, agape, nous*. The mysteries of the macrocosm are within man the microcosm.

> ...*Human body is hard to obtain,*
> *One doth not get it again and again.*
> *When a ripe fruit once falleth from a tree,*
> *Never again doth it return to the branch.*
> **Kabir**

ACKNOWLEDGEMENTS

I wish to thank the following friends and acquaintances who helped with hope and inspiration so that this book may be written:

Helen Fay Whitlock
Dr. Russ Michael
Ro Anne Flora
Wally Ahumada
Dana Walker
Cindy Wallace

CONTENTS

DEATH

The Self or *Atma* never dies, so there has to be another definition of the term 'death'. The *Bhagavad Gita* states that one is never born and never dies. It is the identification of the not-self which undergoes a modification of the change called death. It is the mind with its aggregation of desires which creates the environs for the soul. The mind itself is actually a bundle of various desires (*vasanas*) which form attachments that create the illusory ego. When we first separated from the source we descended first into the domain of the mind. We became confined in the prison house of the world through the bondage of desires.

Having forgotten our divine origin, the awareness of oneness, whatever action the soul performed at the bidding of the mind, wholly involves it with materiality. Earth plane desires and cravings become the fetters for the soul. The body encasement forms the shell which egotism develops. The light of the soul becomes clouded over and the mask of the ego becomes predominant. The mind eventually forgets that the soul is immortal and totally identifies with the body.

The mind is in control of two forces, one centripetal and other centrifugal. The centrifugal energy is outgoing toward the senses and brings identification with the world and becomes attached to desires. The other force is centripetal and is the energy of going within, in meditation toward the soul. Since we predominantly use our mind for outer world activities, our sensory life is greater.

When the soul originally left the divine source, it began to take on a 'body'. The first body it took in its descent to the causal plane was the causal body. In the astral plane upon further descent it took on an astral body. The lower the planes of descent, the greater the illusion; we have the soul immersed in *maya*. This state of *maya* is the illusion of calling a rope a snake. The soul now becomes tied in a knot with the mind. This knot is the nexus of the ego. Ramana Maharshi, the great Indian sage, called this knot the "Granthi knot". The death of the body does not untie this knot. In fact, one can be alive when the knot is untied and be known as a *Jiva-Mukta* or liberated while still in the body.

Ash is a symbol of matter in its most reduced form as no further reduction is possible. During the beginning of the Lenten season, ash is placed on the forehead to remind the Christian of reducing desires and that eventually our bodies will return to ash. Sai Baba materialises *vibhuti* or sacred ash as a potent reminder to give up desire. All things which come together must eventually pull apart. Nothing remains forever, so the important lesson remains in letting go.

The mystery of death is a potent mystery and is tied in with an equally important mystery. Love is another mystery which remains so until the Christ-consciousness is realised. Loving another as oneself is only an ideal and cannot be fully understood until the separated self or ego is conquered. Death is dying to the separated self and will continue to be a reality until one merges into the true Self. The mystery of Christ-consciousness is that we are an individual, a separate unit of consciousness and at the same time one with all that is. When the mind shifts its focus from desires toward the soul, then there is realisation of the all pervasive.

The only thing that dies is appearance. The body is laid to rest or cremated and the appearance of that person in the third dimension ceases to exist. *Sat* or pure existences can never be eliminated, whereas the relative existence of the ego and desires has a limited existence. Law and order can only come from intelligence; divine intelligence is called *chit*.

Because relative existence brings unhappiness from chasing the desires of the ego, true happiness cannot be grasped. *Ananda* or bliss is beyond the relative world and is achieved when one realises his/her immortality.

Mind is the builder. All human dilemmas are the product of the mind. We cannot blame anyone else for our problems. The mind creates stories, plays intellectual games and rationalises behaviour. Our fantasies are projected on to reality. Ego-conflict is caused by emotional and mental obsessions. No one else, especially God, creates our problems. During the course of a lifetime we build up concepts in our mind. At the moment of death, all these concepts—political, economic and racial—all disappear. The only thing that dies is what you thought. Since you are not the concepts or your thoughts, you do not die. Not only are we not our appearance (the body), we are not our thinking process either. Death brings peace. All anxiety and stress ends, all conflicts disappear and all emotion ends.

Our consciousness or belief about a thing makes it so. We cannot remove ourselves from the equation. Even in the realm of science, it is recognised that there is an interplay between the observer and the thing observed. Every thought has a rippling effect, goes out from the thinker and rebounds. There is a whole and implicative order in the universe. There is a rhythm to the universe, *rita*, and we cannot separate ourselves from the whole. One might say that sin is a result of that separation or not being cognisant of it. The laws of the universe are inexorable and have their consequences: yet, everything works together for the good of the whole.

The serpent represents the disintegrating force of cosmic evil which causes the state called death. When we separated from the source, a contraction of identity occurred. Crystallisation builds until death shatters or releases the life within the form.

In Tibetan Buddhism, the belief is that consciousness persists in the subtle state even after breathing has stopped. The mind is light, mobile and very vulnerable in the bardo state. It is not wise to treat the person who is supposedly dead as not being aware of his/her surroundings. The elements of earth dissolve first, then the water element and finally the air element. After the gross elements dissolve, the subtle states of emotion begin to fade. The roots of our desires and anger dissolve and finally we reach the ground luminosity—the *Dharmakaya* or Buddha nature.

One is reminded of the song, "You have to walk through that lonesome valley. No one can do it for you." We are each a prisoner of our own ego. The *vasanas*, or tendencies, are what we acquire in the realm of *samsara* or illusion. Oftentimes, during death or near-death experiences, we see the light as somehow separate from ourselves because of our unfamiliarity with the ground of being. Buddha nature or Christ nature is our real true self.

Death is an opportunity for liberation from the cycle of death and rebirth or the wheel of *samsara*. If you can merge with the light when you first encounter it, then you are liberated. This is the first bardo state. There are subsequent bardo states which lead to other realms and then back to earth again for another birth.

Edgar Cayce taught that our conscious mind passes into our subconscious when we die and upon rebirth we obtain a new conscious mind. In astrology, the moon rules the past life personality which remains in the subconscious. In order to attain full realisation, one has to go through the subconscious. The entire contents of the subconscious have to be emptied before the full superconsciousness can be obtained.

WHEN ARE LIBERATED ALL
The desires that lodge in one's heart,
Then a mortal becomes immortal.

When are cut all
The knots of the heart here on earth,
Then a mortal becomes immortal.
                                        KATHA UPANISHAD

FROM THE UNREAL LEAD ME TO THE REAL
From darkness lead me to light.
From death lead me to immortality.
BRIHADARANYAKA UPANISHAD

THE SEER SEES NOT DEATH,
Nor sickness, nor any distress.
The seer sees only the All,
Obtains the All entirely.
MAITRI UPANISHAD

WHATEVER IS HERE, THAT IS THERE.
What is there, that again is here.
He obtains death after death,
Who seems to see a difference here.

By the mind, indeed, is this [realisation] to be
    attained.
There is no difference here at all!
He goes from death to death,
Who seems to see a difference here.
KATHA UPANISHAD

ETERNITY

Those of us who are bound in time believe eternity to be endless time. Eternity is not endless time, it is timeless. Time has a beginning and an end in relative existence. Herein lies the clue; *Sat*, or pure existence (being), never cannot be. The ultimate ground for *Sat* is *Brahman,* the unknowable. God has no beginning and no end. Who is there to stand behind the ONE knowable? Einstein said that there are two ingredients to measure time: matter and space. There have to be points of reference. *Brahman* fills all space and all matter. There is no place to measure existence which is all pervasive.

The beginning never was and the end will never be. Where does that put us? The answer is *Now.* We always remain in the Now—the Eternal Now. Every moment is now, every day is now, every year is now and every aeon is now. Worlds have come and gone, civilisations have sprung up and crumbled, but *Sat*, or pure existence, forever remains. Therefore, it is existence or eternal existence which also remains a mystery. Division of existence has no meaning.

Socratic inquiry only gives us more questions. Questions cannot produce answers but only bring us to the conclusion at which Socrates himself arrived: he did not know. We do not know that we're perhaps a melody that is being sung by Krishna playing his flute, a dream of Vishnu or a part of Shiva's dance. Deity has many songs to sing, many dreams to dream and many dances to dance just as we will in the course of eternity. All we can say is that we are in the *Now*, between the beginningless beginning and the endless end. We always remain in the middle; all our past and all our so-called future is *Now* which has to be between them both.

We never arrive, we never achieve or reach the goal. From the ego or separate self, it always remains asyntopic; we get closer and closer but never reach the goal. The ego believes itself to be the doer; that is, it initiates a beginning and arrives at a conclusive end. In a dream, time is dilated or expanded. After death, a whole lifetime can be displayed with every thought, feeling and emotion, in just a brief duration. This is the meaning of infinity—you never finish.

Events create the moments; events can be speeded up or slowed down. *Karma* is doing. We are impelled to act in the *now*. Non-action is impossible in the creation. In the creation, nothing rests: atoms are spinning; events are flowing creating time; planets, stars and galaxies are whirling; feeling and thinking continue to flow. It is only the Self, or the ground of being, which remains outside the creation.

> *What is the cause of this universe? Whence do we come? Why do we live? Where shall we at last find rest? Under whose command are we bound by the law of happiness and its opposite?*
>
> *Time, space, law, chance, matter, primal energy, intelligence—none of these, or a combination of these, can be the final cause of the universe, for they are effects, and exist to serve the soul. Nor can the individual self be the cause, for being subject to the law of happiness and misery, it is not free.*
>
> SWETASVATARA UPANISHAD

Symbols used to describe infinity are the ourobouros, the mobius and the lemscate. The first is a snake biting its own tail. This analogy implies a curved universe enfolding upon itself. The mobius similarly is a mathematical model used to describe the same type of enfolding as does the lemscate. In the creation, there is preservation and destruction. Worlds are created, last for a period and then dissolve. These three qualities—creation, preservation and destruction—though aspects of deity, do not constitute the ground of being; *Brahman* subsumes all three.

Who or what is *Brahman?* The ancients referred to *Brahman* as that:

ARISE YE! AWAKE YE!
Obtain your boons [answers] and understand them!
A sharpened edge of a razor, hard to traverse.
A difficult path is this—poets declare!

What is soundless, touchless, formless, imperishable,
Likewise tasteless, constant, odourless,
Without beginning, without end, higher than the great stable.
By discerning That, one is liberated from the mouth of death.

                                        KATHA UPANISHAD

A Buddhist's statement would be, "Emptiness is form, form is emptiness." One cannot know this truth without merging into the ground of one's being. Paradoxes are often used to understand the nouemenal. Immanuel Kant, the German philosopher, knew that paradoxes apply to the nouemenal when trying to relate infinity with the phenomenal or empirical world. We are left with riddles, conundrums and oxymoronic statements. A snake cannot keep on devouring itself as in the ouroboros.

The Unmanifest is pure existence. It alone is. It is the only unity and when manifestation begins duality occurs. One might say creation occurs from a desire to create which is a movement. In the realm of duality, movement would contain an opposite, or the cessation of movement called rest (inertia). This would imply that there are no straight lines in the cosmos or angles. When movement is pulled upon by inertia, then there is a curve. Space is curved. Galaxies spiral and light bends. Everything returns from whence it started forming circles. Circles begin to repel each other and boundaries are set, e.g., orbits, ring pass nots, etc. Relative existence begins with a desire to create. Similarly, we desire to create and set up worlds for ourselves.

The Great Breath, in esoteric teachings, speaks of a period of outbreath of manifestations and an inbreathing called *Pralaya*. There is an end of the world so to speak and the universe, but there comes eventually another breath. No one can go back and trace how many universes have been created, although, there is speculation as to the age of this one.

God is transcendental but enters into the creation as the Christ. Christ is the Word in which all things came into being:

> *The Word was with God in the beginning. Through the Word all things came into being. Not one thing had its being but through this Word.*
> **JOHN 1:3**

The only begotten Son is forever begetting the only begotten. Christ is God in manifestation. The Hindus call this Word Om. It is the cosmic current which pervades the entire creation:

> *In Christ were created all things in heaven and on earth; everything visible and invisible... Before anything was created, Christ existed, and Christ holds all things in unity.*
> **COL. 1:15-17**

The universe was created with sound and light. No other sound but the *Aum* sounded, *Om* contains all sounds. The A is sounded in the throat, the M in the lips and the U is the rolling sound. God is the indweller in the heart. Meditating on the heart is meditation on God. Meditating on a knower of Brahman is also meditating on Brahman. This is worship of the *Istadevta* or favourite form of God, i.e., Jesus, Krishna, Buddha, etc. The Lord accepts all names and forms of God if done with feeling and reverence.

The infinite exists today in human form as Sai Baba. A full avatar or *poorna* avatar is the infinite *Brahman* in human form.

When darkness threatens to overcome the world, the Lord takes human form...

BHAGAVAD GITA

When one sees eternity in things that pass away and Infinity in finite things, then one has pure knowledge.

BHAGAVAD GITA

THE SELF

> *All this is the One Self, this Self is the Universal Self*
>
> MANDUKYA UPANISHAD

The Real Self which dwells in the heart is very small, as small as a grain of mustard; yet, it contains the whole world, the sky and the entire universe. The Self, which is God, the indweller has all the *mahimas* (powers): it is larger than the large, smaller than the small, lighter than the lightest and heavier than the heaviest. The Self is pure existence and consciousness. It is beyond duality or good and evil. Self-luminous, it is truth needing nothing to uphold it, a smokeless fire, an indestructible atom.

One of Sai Baba's adages is, "Each is all"; there are not many selves like yourself or myself but One Self. The proper method of enquiry concerning the Self (*Atma Vichara*) is "Who am I?" This method of Self-enquiry was used by the illumined sage, Ramana Maharshi. As a youth, he had a death experience and fell to the floor. After losing body identification, he began the enquiry, "Who am I?" Whenever someone asks this question, immediately we point to the heart on the right side of the chest. During our waking state, we experience the soul through our gross body. During our sleep state, the soul is experiencing itself through the astral body. Beyond these three states is the *Turiya* state (union with God).

Identification with the not-self (body, emotions, mind) is the ego. The ego believes itself to be the doer. It is like the country bumpkin who goes to see a play in the city and believes in the characterisation of the actors. He gets so swept away in the play, he forgets that behind the scenes exist a director, a choreographer, lighting technicians, etc. We, too, are caught up in the *maya* or illusion of identifying the unreal as the real.

In the *Bhagavad Gita* during the great war *(Mahabharata)*, Arjuna mounted on a chariot represents the personality; the three horses driving the chariot represent the three bodies (physical, astral, mental) with all of their senses being directed outward. Arjuna is in a predicament as he is losing control of the chariot. Behind him stands Krishna (representing the higher Self). Krishna tells Arjuna to give the reins of the chariot to Him. When the disciple turns toward the inner Self, the personality becomes quiescent and the outer senses are no longer rampant.

What are the attributes of the One Self? Those who abide in the Self possess truth, a mind which is poised between the pairs of opposites, possess self-control, purity and devotion to their teacher. There is a steadfastness and a desire for non-attachment. Love *(prema)*, non-violence *(ahimsa)* and a desire for *satsang* (the company of saintly people) are also there. *Avidya* or ignorance is the opposite of these characteristics, abiding in the not-self.

How can we not love God because God is our own Self. God is the nearest of the near and the dearest of the dear. The Self is the source of everything and when we lose contact with our inner Self, then we feel separate from God and duality occurs. The cure for duality is to see God in everyone. Treat our mates as God, our guest as God and even our enemies. Where there is only oneness (the Self) there is no fear.

> *Having pervaded the entire universe with a portion of my Self, I remain.*
>
> BHAGAVAD GĪTA

The universe with everything in it is none other than the outward flow and crystallised form of *Brahman*. How does *Brahman* manifest as the Self? *Karma* is the Self in the realm of duality. In the dual universe, there are all grades of souls in manifestation; however, each is a portion of the divine Self. Man is God and God is man. Sai Baba says that man minus the ego or separated self is God. All created beings will eventually reach perfection. Everyone graduates. Sai Baba declares that it takes 21 blows of the coconut to obtain liberation; the use of this metaphor describes the awakening process to obtain the ultimate goal. In the Theosophical school of thought, which is an exact parallel to Indian thinking, the stages are: involution, evolution and a third stage which is difficult to explain, involving perfection.

The first stage, *tamas* (involution), is the coming down into the dense world. When we emerged from the source we came into the dense molecular, a slow rate of vibration. Next, *rajas*, or the state of unfoldment, begins. Here, the qualities of perfection begin to manifest. This stage is marked by a period of expression. The last stage is the period when the created being comes near to perfection and very close to merging with the Absolute. These three stages, *tamas, rajas* and *sattva*, are known as the three *gunas*. *Tamas* is the stage of darkness, *rajas*—activity, and *sattva*—harmony. The *gunas* permeate all of creation and to reach the Self one has to transcend the three *gunas*. We are, therefore, in the stage of limited existence as long as we are not Self-Realised.

We reach perfection when we obtain the *Turiya* state which is beyond the three. Here, we are in a state of absolute perfection beyond the realm of *Prakriti* or nature. The realm of the Self is *Purusha*. The key is the mind, again as Edgar Cayce reiterates. The mind can go outward toward the *gunas*, nature *(Prakritis)* or inward toward the soul *(Purusha)*. The centrifugal force is the outward force into the area of the senses and the centripetal force leads us inward.

It is all a question of identification. Who am I? Are we the body with its limited expression? Are we the emotions which change fleetingly? Or, are we the mind which, unrestrained, can lead us on a downward path. The mind is the pivotal point which, when conquered, can lead us upward toward the true Self. Objective reality ceases when the mind ceases to function. Meditation means no mind; that is, the meditator stops the world literally when he stops his mind. Without thoughts, mind cannot exist. However, it is not that easy if one does not practise meditation. When the Self is realised, objective reality disappears.

THE SEPARATE NATURE OF THE SENSES,
and that their arising and setting
is of things that come into being apart
    [from himself],
The wise man recognises, and sorrows not.

Higher than the senses is the mind;
Above the mind is the true being.
Over the true being is the Great Self
    [intellect];
Above the Great is the Unmanifest.

Higher than the Unmanifest, however, is the Person.
All-pervading and without any mark whatever.
Knowing which, a man is liberated
And goes to immortality.

His form is not to be beheld.
No one soever sees Him with the eye.
He is framed by the heart, by the thought, by the mind.
They who know that become immortal.
                                    KATHA UPANISHAD

ENLIGHTENMENT

One cannot be a knower of mysteries until one is illumined. Whether we approach the great unknown through the Eastern or Western tradition, we still have to become enlightened. God-Realisation or Cosmic-Consciousness can be approached through *samadhi* in its various stages. The Christ-Consciousness can be obtained through Western discipleship.

Yoga (union) is a discipline whereby one can reach *samadhi* or union with the Self through *tapas* [austerity and other disciplines: *pranayama* (control of breath), focus on the third eye, etc.] The *savikalpa* stage of *samadhi* is marked by a differentiation between the object perceived and the perceiver. In the *nirvakalpa* stage the object perceived and the perceiver become one. Most of all the disciplines require a lot of work and austerity; however, the easiest path is *Bhakti* (love). This only requires a pure heart dedicated to the Lord and is best approached in the *Kali Yuga* by repeating the name of the Lord. The other path, *Jnana Marga* (the path of wisdom) requires much more effort. Yogananda used to say that if you loved God enough He would reveal everything to you.

> *THE WISE FULL OF LOVE WORSHIP ME*
> *believing that I am the origin of all*
> *and that moves on through me.*

> *Placing their minds on me,*
> *offering their lives to me,*
> *instructing each other and speaking about me*
> *they are always happy and contented.*
> *To these who are constantly devoted*
> *and who worship with love*
> *I give that knowledge by which they attain to me.*
> *And remaining in their hearts,*
> *I destroy with the brilliant lamp of knowledge*
> *the darkness born of ignorance in such men only*
> *Out of compassion for them.*
>
> **BHAGAVAD GITA**

Enlightenment is merging into the infinite consciousness, into the Void, into the great silence where there is no perceiver or object perceived. There is no subconscious, consciousness or unconsciousness. The Christian mystics would call it "a rich naught". Only a human being is given the ability to reach this magnificent state. This is how precious a human birth is. The body is used as a boat to cross the ocean of *samsara*.

Sai Baba explains that nowhere else in the entire universe is it possible, except here on earth, to attain this full realisation. Even the gods have to obtain human birth to reach the ultimate awareness of *Brahman*. This makes the human body and earth a very special place.

Obviously, we are talking about the very highest state of consciousness. There has never been a civilisation where everyone in society achieved Cosmic-Consciousness. It could also be said that it would be difficult to live in society in such a high level of consciousness. We are used to functioning with our ego intact. Whenever you are not, the Divine is present. Wherever you are, the Divine is absent. You might say that the goal is to become nobody. The Christian would exclaim, "not me but Christ in me." In the Zen teachings it would be expressed, "Chopping wood and carrying water but no one is present."

There are three things which will inhibit the higher consciousness: *kama* (lust), *krodha* (anger) and *lobha* (greed). The Holy Spirit will not abide with you if any of these three are present. This is why all traditions require a period of discipleship before initiation is given into the inner teachings. There is a cost of discipleship. In fact, the Indian tradition parallels the Christian Western tradition. *Brahmacharya* (celibacy) is common to both; although, in this new age, the *grihastha* (householder) path is allowed. Humility is also a prerequisite which is why *seva* or service is so important. You might say all the virtues should be prevalent in the *sadhaka* or disciple.

Once the necessary disciplines are a part of the disciple, the master, guru or teacher will bring the *chela*, student, closer to the goal. One of the injunctions on the spiritual path is "to make haste slowly." Spirit is a fire and can destroy as well as elevate. *Kundalini* should be aroused slowly, and the ego should be purified of all lower tendencies. Other prescriptions for the spiritual path are: silence, eating small quantities of food, *ahimsa* (non-violence), faith, cleanliness, studying scripture, *satsang* (company of saints) and *tapas* (spiritual discipline).

Enlightenment may come suddenly; however, that may be due to merit from previous births. A *bhastra* is a *yogi* who almost attained liberation in his previous life but did not quite make the grade. One simply picks up where one left off. We are all phantoms on the physical plane as each of us does not know nor can gauge the evolution of another soul. The silent watchers guard and guide humanity and know how far we have come.

Unto the initiates is given to know the mysteries, and enlightenment cannot be given freely unless one has earned it. Even an evil person can reverse his negative *karma* and attain liberation in the same life. An example is Milerapa, who, through following his guru's advice, attained the final goal. God is the silent witness who sees deeply into the heart of each soul and rewards us accordingly. Also, *karma* can be forgiven through sincere repentance and a change of heart and mind (*metanoia*).

Mysteries are revealed slowly usually because each step has to be mastered. There is no such thing as failure, only loss of time. Nature is slow to reveal her secrets and rightly so. Right vision is important and everything is holy since God is the source of all.

Something should be said about *Sankalpa* (will). We are bombarded by a myriad of thoughts every day, and it is so important to choose the right thoughts. We are responsible for the choices we make in life and the will leads us or misleads us in whatever situation we find ourselves; therefore, watchfulness or vigilance is another spiritual attribute to acquire. If we guard our thoughts, we guard our soul. One merely has to look at the expressions on people's faces as an indication of what kind of thoughts they have.

God-Consciousness is our birthright. No one is barred who turns his attention Godward. *Sat-Chit-Ananda* is our normal condition, not a state of asleepness:

THE CARPENTER SINGING HIS AS HE MEASURES HIS PLANK OR BEAM.
The shoemaker singing as he sits on his bench.
The hatter singing as he stands.
The delicious singing of the mother or of the young wife at work...
Singing with open mouths their strong melodious songs...
I bestow upon any man or woman the entrance to all the gifts of the universe.
                                                        WALT WHITMAN

LOVE

> *The lotus on the lake is far, far away from the sun;
> but distance is no bar for the dawn of love; the
> lotus blooms as soon as the sun peeps over the
> horizon.*
>
> **SATHYA SAI BABA**

Everything comes alive under the gaze of the sun and so it is
under the gaze of love. Love is also a great mystery as no one
can explain it fully because no one can fully explain God.
There was no one to know the original Divine Person until He
created everything. Having come out of Himself, He gave it
His love (Son). He spoke the Word *(Aum)* and immediately all
came into being. Love is all that there is because in the
beginning there was just the Word. Since there was no one to
know Him, He created the All for his pleasure *(leela)* or divine
sport. The ultimate mystery then is God wanting to know
Himself. Love is seeking love and reflecting it back on itself.

> *The countless gods are only my million faces.*
>
> **BHAGAVAD GITA**

Selflessness, not selfishness, is the essence of love. A
hater of beings is a very selfish person. When one does not
want to give selflessly, then that person does not know how to
truly love. Love is not giving with the hope to receive but just
giving unselfishly. We are all inextricably bound by ties of love.

Sometimes we see this divine quality in animals. A rat has been known to lead its blind mate with a straw. Birds sometimes leave their flock to be with a mate who is injured in some way. The devotion of a dog to his master is legendary and even a wild animal responds to kindness by attaching itself to a good Samaritan.

Love is the cohesive force which binds molecules of matter together. It is the unifying force behind creation, and yes, even inanimate objects respond to love. When food is prepared with love, everyone who eats of it is blessed. The food given by the guru is called *prasad* as it is imbued with his grace and love.

Every Christian is told to love one another. We know that we have passed out of death into life, because we love the brethren (I John 3:14). If we are all to become members of the same spiritual body (the body of Christ), then we are known by that love. If God's love is absent, there can be no brotherly love. Simply, we are able to love others because God first loved us.

The concept of a soul mate is interesting because when we encounter one, we are automatically drawn to that person like a magnet. The attraction transcends personality differences because the resonance is on a deeper spiritual level. We are always united with our soul mate on the soul plane but sometimes encounter our soul mate in this dimension. A good book to read on this subject is *Finding Your Soul Mate* by Russ Michael published by Weiser Books.

True love can only be love of God. What we call love on the earth plane is conditional love. We love our parents because they took care of us in our youth: however, as they age many times they are warehoused in nursing homes. Love for siblings, mates and friends is also conditional. Our love on this earth is tinged with selfishness. We even have a sense of possessiveness as if we owned each other. Once we transcend our ego by selfless service and humility, then we can truly love as we see the One behind the many.

Sai Baba reminds us that the only religion is love; the only caste is humanity. Each is all, so there should not be anyone who is not deserving of our love. Even evil individuals have the spark of divinity in them and should be loved—however, not the evil they do. Eventually, everyone returns to the ocean of bliss, however, many lives it takes or hell worlds they attend. Because we live in the realm of duality, we cannot see the omnipresent divinity as *maya* clouds our vision; therefore, it is incumbent upon each of us to correct our vision.

Western scientific materialism will not reach the goal in ascertaining the infinite. Physics and chemistry belong in the realm and dominion of the senses. The senses are true in the empirical world but cannot penetrate spirit. A Russian biologist once helped a small Siberian animal, binding its wounds and returning it back to its natural habitat. When she returned home, many hundreds of miles away, she found the animal waiting there for her. The loving kindness she showed the animal became a beacon for the animal to follow. The scientist wanted to dissect the animal to discover what chemicals were operating to cause the animal to find her. They will never find the cause since they lack the understanding of the love principle involved.

Truly the way to God is love. "Start the day with love, live the day with love, end the day with love. This is the way to God" (Sathya Sai Baba). *Bhakti* is devotion, worshipping God with true feeling. No act of prayer or worship should be performed without deep reverence and feeling. Love is the highest law and supersedes *karma*. *Karma* is the old "eye for an eye". If you are to die in this incarnation because in the past life you took a life, you can apply the higher law of love and save a life, therefore balancing the *karma*. There is an old story about Jesus walking with his disciples and they observed a woodcutter about to enter the woods. The master spoke to his disciples and said, "If that woodcutter knew that this would be the last day of his life today, he would not be whistling and in such a happy mood." At the end of the day the disciples reminded their master that no ill had befallen the woodcutter.

The master replied, "Indeed, today was to be the day of his demise, but as the woodcutter journeyed he came upon a man dying and bleeding from wounds obtained from a wild beast, so he ministered to the dying man, bandaging his wounds and giving him food and drink. Because of that act of mercy, the Lord spared his life." Love is the fulfilling of the law.

IF, WITH LOVE ONE STRETCHES OUT TO ME
A leaf, a blossom, fruit, or water
I take from that devoted soul
The heart-given offering.

Whatever you do, whatever you eat
Whatever you give, whatever you offer
Whatever austerities you undergo,
... do it as an offering to me.

Thus you will be released,
From the bonds of action, its fair and evil fruits,
Your self trained in the discipline of denial.
Freed, you will move swiftly to me.

I am the same in all beings,
No one is hateful or dear to me,
But those who turn to me with love
Are in me, and I too am in them.

BHAGAVAD GITA

THE FATHER

The Trinity is indeed a great mystery. The three are in One and the One is in the three. The Father, the Son and the Holy Spirit (Christian); Shiva, Vishnu and Brahma (Hindu); or Aumakua, Uhane and Unihiphlif (Hawaiian). All trinitarian religions are based on the One dividing into three. The One subsumes the other two. Hear this story: The two gods, Vishnu and Brahma, were having a debate as to which one was the greatest. Immediately, a great pillar of fire arose between them and it was Shiva who contained them both.

The Father aspect (Shiva) of the trinity contains all three. Before the One divided, it remained only One. First there had to be the will to be. The Father is omnipotent and His power gives life and vivifies. It is the Father aspect of the Trinity which gives purpose, synthesis and intention to all things. Our direction and purpose come from the Father aspect. Without the Father aspect of God, we would not be impelled to action, there would be no purpose in life, and we would not be impelled to initiate anything.

Sai Baba is Shiva and Shakti: that is, Mother (Sai) and Father (Baba). He is the mother and father of all. God the Father is the power aspect of his being. His will is Absolute and must be accomplished. Actually there is only free will to a relative degree since the Absolute will must prevail over all.

Individually, the power aspect of God (Father) resides in the *atma* of man. Man is an individualised spark of God and can exercise his *sankalpa* or will. Whenever we focus our entire attention on an ideal, we bring all of our power to bear—our personality, our mind and our feeling into a one-pointed direction. Much can be accomplished when one's *atma* or will is mobilised. Sai Baba's will is so absolute that he can materialise in a moment whatever he wills into manifestation: *vibhuti* (sacred ash) rings, necklaces, food, etc. Since he is *premaswarupa* (embodiment of love) he does all of this, through his *sankalpa*, but the motivating force is love.

The power of God is there as a motivating force and is transcendent as well as established in this dimension. One must understand this power and not be solely concerned with its material application exclusively; otherwise, it will be difficult to understand its universal application. We live in a vast sea of consciousness, and when we remain unconscious of spiritual power it remains inchoate. We must consciously remind ourselves that we are an integral part of the cosmos and our brain is constantly sending out its signals which in turn has an effect on all that is. Physicists have recognised a whole implicate order to the universe which parallels this spiritual reality.

The Father creates through divine mind and his creations have life. We cannot create and give life except as we energise our thought forms and give them life. We can manipulate matter, rearrange it but lack the capacity to create. The power of God is the real power in man and is revealed through His Son/Sun. The Father is life, the Son ensouls and the Mother nurtures. Life is created for a *purpose*. This is the mystery of humility. All forms and names of God were brought into being for His pleasure and by His will. All life has value and a reason for *being*, *Sat* is truth, pure existence or beingness which makes all life sacred. We should respect this sanctity that is in all of the many forms of God. Without this power, nothing could come into being and we are all held in the mind of God as His perfect creations.

It is the Father aspect which knows the *intention* or will and purpose of being. As the drama of life is played out on the stage of *maya* in this relative existence, the real purpose of being lies deep within the *atma* of every *jiva* or soul. God's first law is forward progression (evolution) and everything moves along according to His will. What apparently looks like regression is merely the working out of the law of *karma* (lessons).

In a large sense, this will is seen working out as the spirit of the nation or collective will. You might say that destiny is largely associated with the spirit or will-to-become. As evolution progresses, the sense of purpose changes to accommodate the higher intention. The Father aspect is Omnipotence, the Mother aspect is Omniscience and the Son is Omnipresence.

What is it that can cause galaxies to spiral, suns to ignite and life to permeate the entire cosmos? Such power can only come from the Almighty. As a spark of the Divine, this same power resides in each one of us. We are never apart from this Presence, but sometimes have to remind ourselves that we are a part of the whole. The great mystery of the Trinity resides within man—the microcosm. The Father aspect resides in the top of the head where the *sutratma* or thread to the God-Self beats down. The Son (Christ) resides between the eyes (*ajna*) and is called the star of the east. The Holy Spirit is located in the medulla area behind the head. This is the reason the head area is protected in many religions: e.g., Islam, Judaism, etc. During infancy, the neonate has a large soft spot (fontanelle) on the top of the head. As we grow and develop this opening gradually closes until the Saturn return, approximately $28\frac{1}{2}$ years. Saturn, in astrology, is the Father aspect. It is the Father who impels life to grow, live and flourish until we reach maturity where we can define our own lives.

The historical Christ began his mission during His Saturn return. He was in constant union with the Father (*Abba* or *Baba*). His human will merged with cosmic will and He went about His Father's business. The will is the intention and He taught that we can discern intention by the fruits. Whatever *sankalpa* or intention is can be revealed by the fruits of expression. Oftentimes, we can discern intention by the expression in people's eyes or facial expressions. Eventually, we all live what we truly believe, and manifest in our lives the fruits of our *sankalpas* (will).

It is important to remember that whatever is not in alignment with cosmic will is destroyed. This is the Shiva-Nataraj aspect of God as destroyer. What is destroyed, however, is the limiting factor which does not move the life aspect forward.

> *Behold, I am the destroyer of forms.*
> **OPPENHEIMER QUOTING HINDU SCRIPTURE**

On this planet, the Will of God is located in Shamballa, an etheric retreat in the Gobi Desert where all perfected beings reside. The energy of Shamballa is manifest in the discovery of the atomic bomb. This is the physical aspect of power. As we get closer to the end of the Piscean Age, this aspect of God will become more manifested, i.e., earthquakes, upheavals, etc. This destruction is always prevalent when a world cycle comes to a close in preparation for a new birth. Therefore, it is incumbent upon each of us to get in alignment with cosmic will and purpose. The safest way to do this is to follow the path of *dharma* or righteousness. *Dharma* is right *karma*.

The best example of perfect alignment of oneness with cosmic will is Jesus's prayer in the Garden of Gethsemane. Edgar Cayce sheds light on this subject in his discourses.

> Q.   *What is the difference between desire of the heart and desire of the will?*
> A.   *Only in Him. In speaking of the heart and of the will, analyse for the moment as to what they represent in thine own experience. The heart is ordinarily considered the seat of life in the physical, while the will is a motivating factor in the mental and spiritual realm.*

To be sure, these may be made one. But how? In that the will of the self and the desire of the heart are selfless in the Christ-Consciousness. Even as He gave in the shadow of the day when the Cross loomed before Him on Calvary, when the desire of the heart and the will of self were made one. Indeed, as He gave, the flesh is weak, the spirit is willing... For, the soul is in Him, yet, as the promise of Christ is, the soul shall be free in Him through that love, through the manner of making the desire and the will one in the Father as He did in Gethsemane.

EDGAR CAYCE 262-64

THE SON

The second aspect of the Trinity is the mystery of Christ, the saviour or redeemer.

> *If I be lifted up, shall draw all men to me.*
> **JESUS CHRIST**

Whereas the Father aspect is the mind of God, the Son is the heart—representing love-wisdom. In Buddhism, the saviour or redeemer is called the *Bodhisattva*; in Hinduism, the preserver or Vishnu.

In the plant kingdom, the rays of the sun draw the young seedlings upward and the plants utilise the sun's rays to process their food through photosynthesis. The sun (son) gives light and love. When the energy comes from the Father and pours through the Son, the will aspect becomes goodwill: love to all beings. This love is what creates brotherhood of all men under one Father.

Omnipresence is the quality of the Son. Other aphorisms are the light of the world, the teacher of teachers, the saviour and the divine mystery. Since the One fragmented itself, each of the sparks of the Divine are seeking individualisation. You might say that we are all individualised sons of God: however, we have to seek this relationship as did Jesus the Christ.

At the time of Jesus, the Piscean Age, the fish was a potent symbol. Those who were to become fishers of men were the leaders of that 2000-year dispensation. In the opposite sign Virgo, the Virgin holding a sheaf of wheat, the mysteries of healing were revealed. Jesus multiplied loaves and fishes which symbolised both signs.

In the Aquarian Age, we are to witness the maturity of man. This age promises rapid development in the affairs of men. The opposite sign Leo will reveal another potent mystery—the Son (Sun) or Son of man. All of the ancient mysteries pointed to the birth of the Sun. This mystery has to do with the perfection of man. The time of man's perfection could only come now in the Aquarian Age, the Age of Man and the Sun (Son of man).

Divine wisdom, the Son of the Father, took on flesh and became man in human flesh. This primordial light existed before the foundation of the world. The Christ light is universal and no one sect or religion can claim it exclusively. There will always be sons of the sons as the only begotten is forever begetting the only begotten.

The Son is the light of consciousness—the universal awareness through the light of love-wisdom which binds all things together in the whole. Love is the magnet which draws all opposites together in perfect unity. The first love we should have is the love of the Son for the father which is eloquently written in the "Shema", Heb. for "listen".

> *Hear, O Israel, the Lord our God is One Lord; and you shall love the Lord, your God, with all your heart and with all your soul, and with all your might...*

We have both a human nature and a divine nature. The divine nature remains a hidden nature until we cultivate it. We have to believe in the Son of God and pass through the second birth. In Hinduism it is called twice born. The heart and the mind are fused, whereas there is intelligence in the heart and love in the mind. The Baptism is the beginning of the stream toward the Christ-Consciousness. The windows of heaven begin to open and a new and higher level of understanding is attained. The Prodigal Son has returned home.

Next is the Transfiguration; then the mind is illumined with the Christ light and the personality begins to shine forth its radiance. Once the mind is turned toward the Self, then Ascension or liberation is assured. The Crucifixion follows and the separated self is swallowed up in the divine Self. In Buddhism one is called an *Arhat* and in Hinduism, a *Paramahamsa*.

All celestial sons of God are true representatives of the Father and seek to only do His will. The Creation continues to sing and awaits all prodigals to return home. It does not matter one iota what religion or caste one belongs to as long as that love is prevalent.

The ancient name for India is *Bharata*—lovers of the Lord—which is why it is the destiny of this country to always be the world teacher. Many avatars have incarnated there throughout history: Rama, Krishna, Buddha and the present day Sai Baba. The avatar behaves in a human way so that we may feel kinship within Him and then rises to superhuman heights so that we may aspire to do the same. This Sai avatar has come to restore the *dharma* as it is in the *Sanatana Dharma*, the ancient highway to God. In previous ages, the avatar came to destroy the enemies of the *dharma*. Now, in this age of *Kali* (darkness), no one is pure. Rather than destroy, this avatar will correct man's *buddhi* or intelligence, bring peace in the world and help man transcend his ego.

Interiorising the Christ light is the goal of every initiate on the path. At a certain stage of evolution, a sun-like light becomes awakened in the individual. This is depicted in the 16th chapter in the *Book of Isaiah*.

> *The sun shall be no more thy light by day; neither for brightness shall the moon give light unto thee: but the Lord shall be unto thee an everlasting light, and thy God thy glory.*
>
> *Thy sun shall no more go down; neither shall thy moon withdraw itself: for the Lord shall be thine everlasting light, and the days of thy mourning shall be ended.*

The sun within man is his highest spiritual Self, his monad, which is right above him. Once this radiance is contacted within, the initiate begins to glow like the sun. Much of the *Bible* is written in allegory or parable and contains much hidden wisdom.

Though there be many stars in the heavens, many suns, there is only one flame which sets them all aglow, the Sacred Fire. One of the best books on this subject is *Treatise on Cosmic Fire* by Alice A. Bailey (Lucis Trust). This fire also has to do with the alchemical tradition which teaches the transmutation of lead into gold. It is actually in man in which this phenomenon occurs. Mercury (the mind) is the key. "If thine eye is single, the whole body is turned into light." In contradistinction, if the mind is focused on darkness, how great is the darkness? Do not move on the path with gloom and despair. You should know that the real you is deathless and will arise like a phoenix. Just as when the sun goes down in the evening, it arises the next day. Even in primitive ages past, the sun was a constant reminder of the dispeller of darkness. Once even a small candle is lit, all the darkness in the room disappears. Actually, darkness does not exist— darkness is only the absence of light. One of the aphorisms of Christ is "the Son of Righteousness, with healing in its wings." The winged solar disc was also used in Egypt depicting Osiris.

This mystery will continue to unfold in the Aquarian/Leo Age. The oldest prayer in the world alludes to the Great Central Sun in the *Gayatri* prayer.

O THOU WHO GIVES SUBSTANCE
To the whole universe,
From Whom all things proceed,
To Whom all things return,
Unveil to us the face of the

True Spiritual Sun
Hidden by a dish of golden light
So that we may do our whole·duty
As we journey to Thy sacred feet.

THE MOTHER

The purpose of the Mother aspect of God is the nurturing of life forms and the guidance of intelligent activity. Once the Christ is born as a child, it needs a mother. The soul or seeker on the spiritual path needs to be nurtured.

> DARK MOTHER! *ALWAYS GLIDING NEAR WITH SOFT FEET;*
> *Have none chanted for thee, a chant of fullest*
> *welcome?*
>
> **WALT WHITMAN**

In the realm of duality, light and shadow, the soul has taken on the vesture of flesh, blood and bones. Nature, the mother, periodically changes her clothes at different seasons. The Hindus are often accused of having many gods; however, it is their many-faceted symbol of the one God they admire. God is often seen in an anthropomorphic way in many of the world's religions. If there is a man sitting on the throne, then there must be a woman also.

The soul in the material body is gobbled up in time, the *Kali-chakra*. The vision of *Kali* is horrible, suffering without end. As everyone knows, in nature life eats up life. To the Hindus, the soul is *purush* and nature is *prakriti*. This is the dance of Shiva and Shakti.

In the Piscean/Virgo Age, there is the Madonna and her Child. This potent symbol has many meanings, one of which the mother holds the key to the recurrence of divine forms in creation. These forms house the inner light, just as our physical vehicle carries our soul. The darkness of matter is the womb from which we all emerge into this world. You might say that we are always going from darkness to light in birth after birth.

The soul plays a feminine role toward the Self; that is, it must submit itself like a bride to the groom. The wedding garment is the divine Sophia and here is the preparation necessary to merge with the Self. Receptivity is the key to the Mother aspect of God. The mother is receptive, responsive and nurturing. The disciple has to submit to the higher life which in all traditions requires prayer, meditation, silence, etc. This is why, in the Catholic Church, prayer to Mary helps in that receptivity.

> *A great sign appeared in the sky, a woman clothed with the sun, with the moon under her feet, and on her head a crown of twelve stars.*
> **REVELATION 12:1**

In order to understand the feminine mysteries, every initiate has to understand the balance of the masculine and feminine within him or her self. Every world religion has the divine feminine: Quan Yin in China, Isis in Egypt, Gaia in Greece, and Mary in Christianity. In Taoism, it is the balance of Yin (magnetic) with Yang (electric) forces. These two forces are centripetal and centrifugal.

Luna, in astrology, represents the subconscious forces, Illumination or Christhood requires the blending of the two, conscious and subconscious, as taught in the Christian mysteries.

The cross in Christian terms represents the two forces coming together; the vertical (masculine) and the horizontal (feminine). At the point where they meet is the rosy cross or awakened heart *chakra*. Sai Baba speaks of the cross as a symbol whereby the small 'I' of the ego is cut across or negated, so the larger Self will come forth.

Jesus's mother Mary represents the divine feminine in the fullest sense. The name itself often refers to the "sea" which alludes to the feminine aspect of the subconscious. There are three aspects to her divine feminine role: the virgin, the mother, and the wise woman. She is the divine model of the illumined soul (feminine) giving birth to the Christ within. As the wise woman, she is the divine Sophia (wisdom). Mary is present at every birth on earth.

There are always embodiments of the divine Mother on earth at any given time. Today, in India, Sai is the mother to all beings. One of his missions is to give love to all beings who have never known the love of a mother. Another incarnation was Anandamayima who has recently passed on. Other models of the feminine aspect of God living today are Mother Meera, Mother Teresa, Mataji and many others.

In one of Mary's prayers known as Mary's Canticle, the aspects of the divine feminine are clearly revealed. This is found in the first chapter of Luke:

> *My soul doth magnify the Lord: And my spirit rejoices in God my Saviour, For He has regarded the lowliness of this handmaid. And behold, from henceforth all generations shall call me blessed. For He that is mighty doth great things for me and holy is His name. And His mercy is from generation unto generation to them that fear Him. He hath shown might with His arm. And He hath scattered the proud in the conceit of their heart. He hath put down the mighty from their throne and has exalted the lowly. He hath filled the hungry with good things, and the rich He hath sent away empty. He hath received Israel, His servant, being mindful of His mercy. As He spoke to our fathers, to Abraham and to His seed forever.*
>
> **LUKE 1:46-55**

The lesson of the divine feminine in this canticle is a formula for each of us to be receptive to the spirit as she was in the time of the Annunciation. The feminine principle represents the subconscious which is the repository of the soul. On the inward path, it is the feminine aspect of the soul which must yield to the Self or god-being.

The world comes into being through Shakti, the mother principle. In Shaivism, which stems from the matriarchal relationship of the Mother Goddess (*devi*) Shakti is energy. Shiva is normally considered to be consciousness or spirit and Shakti, his consort, is His power. It is Shiva, the ascetic who is in a state of meditation or contemplation of the whole universe, and Shakti who moves the universe around. All the energy of the universe appears as a point (*bindu*) and expands in an outward fashion. You might say out of nothing a concentrated point of energy appears. The energy comes out of the point in triangles and squares; that is, the Mother gives birth to forms. The mathematical or geometric pattern is what is referred to in *Tantra* as a *Yantra*. In certain Hindu temples, there are *yantras* of great power which, when meditated upon, link one up with the structure of the whole universe. Man, the miniature universe, has his *bindu* on the top of his head from which emerges his *chakras*, whirling forces, and it is Shakti which energises his being also. The whole dance of the cosmos is the marriage of Shiva and Shakti.

The *kundalini* energy, coiled like a serpent, at the base of the spine rising up, is really the goddess herself moving up the *chakras* seeking to unite with Shiva at the top of the crown. Shiva is the One and Shakti is the many. "The One thing has become ten thousand things"—Taoism.

THE ASCENSION

> *For the Lord Himself shall descend from heaven*
> *with a shout, with the voice of the archangel, and*
> *with the trump of God: and the dead in Christ shall*
> *rise first: then we which are alive and remain shall*
> *be caught up together with them in the clouds, to*
> *meet the Lord in the air: and so shall we ever be*
> *with the Lord.*
>
> **I THESSALONIANS 4**

The key to understanding what Paul is saying here is in the "air"—accurately describing the ascension from the dense molecular vibration of flesh, blood and bones, to the more rarefied ethers of the soul. Spiritual realities cannot be proven by physical facts. The laws of the physical creation (science) are true in the realm and dimension of the empirical world of the senses or *indriyas*. However, spiritual realities do show through and manifest through the physical, and it is the current of life which penetrates through and the intensity of that current which indicates how strong the spirit will manifest.

> *Clasp the ten indriyas together and merge the*
> *Jivatma with the Paramatma.*
>
> **SAI BABA**

In the sixth century, before Christ and the Buddha, there was a breakthrough in consciousness with the *Upanishads*.

Since that time in India, adepts pierced the veil of the senses. Long before America and the Soviet Union went into outer space, India had conquered inner space. This conquest of inner space, or adventures in consciousness, led to the discovery of the ultimate reality—*Brahman*. It is much harder to penetrate the subtle dimensions by mechanical means: e.g., virtual reality, hyperspace, etc., than by direct inner perception. Man contains within himself subtle bodies, *kosas*, which cannot be replicated by physical means alone. In the West, we are trying to move from the outer reality to the inner, but the East has already moved from the inner reality to the outer.

Around 500 B.C. we see from the *Katha Upanishad* how the foundation of the universe and human consciousness was comprehended at this time, "Beyond the senses (*indriyas*) is *manas*, or the mind. Beyond the mind is the intellect, or *buddhi*. Beyond the intellect is *mahat*, or great Self. Beyond *mahat* is the unmanifest—*aryakta* and beyond the unmanifest is *purusha*. The lowest level of the mind is the senses. The senses chain us to the desires of the physical world, hence, the wheel of *samsara* or illusion."

Later on in the fourth century, St. Augustine was quoted as saying:

> *That which is called the Christian religion existed among the ancients from the beginning of the human race; at the coming of Christ Jesus, true religion began to be called Christianity.*

Most people think of the Ascension as a solitary act done by Lord Jesus, when, in fact, masters and adepts of different world religions have performed likewise. Sri Yukteswar appeared to his disciples on the sands of Puri. (See *Autobiography of a Yogi* by Paramahamsa Yogananda.) Ramakrishna appeared in a light body to his disciples as well. Lao Tse ascended while sitting on an ox. The Sufis call the Ascension a translation into the electronic world. Even today among some initiates, the Ascension is still a reality. This is not a mystery as it is a part of every man's life. As with every other accomplishment there must be a preparation. There are two stages in this preparation. First, there is in this New Age a new body (vehicle) being built. We must prepare for this new body by preparing our mind to accept the light.

> *Be transformed by the renewing of your mind.*
> PAUL

Man will no longer have a gross physical body and a spiritual body but a fusion of both. Heaven and earth are coming together due to the influx of the seventh ray pouring into the solar system—the Aquarian ray. The seventh ray is the lowest densification of the light. Once the physical and the spiritual bodies unite, the new man will be a different creature. Since the physical world is the world of effect and not cause, for the Ascension to take place, the spiritual must be the beginning. Mind is the builder, so the preparation must start with mind control. The *indriyas* are gathered up and controlled by the mind which then begins the process of illumination from within. Once the light is contacted, then one must spend at least an hour a day to imbibe this Christ light and let it course through the whole body.

A simple technique is *dhyana*, meditation, as recommended by Sri Sathya Sai Baba. Find a quiet place to meditate, preferably at the same time and place, and begin with a lit candleflame. Meditate on that *jyoti*, lighted flame, in your heart. Imagine the light of this flame penetrating your whole body, sending this light out from you to the world, to loved ones, friends, enemies, etc. By this simple technique, the dross or affect of negation from the body will be removed. As the negative patterns of thought and feeling are removed from the body, a new and lighter body will begin to manifest. By letting go of all preconceived thought patterns in the body and allowing the Christ light to penetrate, you then bring about the actual existence of the new man.

Once this is accomplished, you then bring about what the ancient mystics called the alchemical marriage, whereby the body and the mind are prepared for the Ascension. There is no mystery when it is understood that the rate of vibration of the body is enhanced and it is like walking from one room (rate of vibration) to another room (higher rate of vibration).

Sai Baba confounds scientists by materialising objects with his *sankalpa* or will. He states that whatever is invisible can be made visible and that which is visible can be rendered invisible. Spirit is matter when cognised by the senses and matter is spirit at a much faster rate of vibration.

The Ascension is the culmination or fulfilment of this process. When the light fills every cell in the body, the substance or *sub-stance* is caused to move at a much faster rate of vibration, by the life and light being infused. The difference between the two states of matter is the pulsations in the matter. It is the amount of spirit infused into matter which renders or causes all forms to exist. What you call the world around you is perceived by your consciousness which in turn interprets the vibrations of the material world. This spirit or force exists in the human nervous system, which in man is higher than other forms. You can call this energy electrical nerve fluid if you like. The Oriental call it *Chi* and the Indians *prana*. It is vibration which causes matter to change. Once the disciple activates this vibration he or she becomes radioactive and starts emitting energy. This is the life-force seeking a higher life wave. The mineral becomes the plant; the plant becomes the animal; the animal becomes man, man becomes the angel, etc.

Ascension is an upward spiral in evolution all ascending to where life came from. Compounds are constantly breaking up forming new compounds in an endless array of differing forms of manifestation, all leading to the one ocean of life. Ultimately, one has to go beyond the order of gods, goddesses, angels, etc., to the uncreated. In Hinduism, this is called the *Nirguna Brahman* or world of the uncreated, without attributes. In the *Saguna*, or world of the created,

God appears as a Person. In the Christian tradition, the *nirguna* state is called the Godhead; Buddhism calls this *Sunyata*. Beyond darkness, beyond light is called the great void. Here, there is no body, no separateness, no individuality, only the ineffable. One must not get the impression that at any step in the raising of consciousness can one omit any of the lower levels. It is the gathering up of all levels of consciousness that one must ascend through. When one reaches the Supreme, all the levels of reality are embraced. This is called *sahaja samadhi*. The avatar is in a constant state of *sahaja samadhi*—appearing in this world but aware of all levels of creation.

> *The eye has no access there, nor has speech nor mind; we so not know It (The Absolute), nor the method whereby we can impart It. It is other than the known as well as the unknown: so indeed do we hear from the sages of old who explained It thus to us.*
>
> KENO UPANISHAD

This explanation of matter from the dense to the less dense is the order in the cosmic scale of creation. All matter including the composition of our bodies is under the control of the mind. The Ascension, therefore, is climbing up the stairway of the ladder of creation by means of rate of vibration. The entire cosmic physical plane is the backdrop of the cosmic astral plane which in turn is the backdrop of the cosmic mental plane until we get to the first cause.

One can transcend the relative world of cause and effect by practising *karma yoga*; that is, doing one's duty in the world and surrendering the fruits thereof. It is important to remember that we are not the doer. God is the indweller who performs all actions through us.

Another way is *bhakti* (love) yoga whereby one's full and complete devotion to the Lord acts as a magnet which draws us closer to Him. Paramahamsa Yogananda once said, "If you love the Lord enough, He will reveal Himself to you."

Om Shanti, Shanti Shantih!

KARMA

That which is called *karma* is otherwise called the law of manifestation; that is, whatever seeks to manifest does so through the process of involution and evolution. This orderly process is merely the natural law of cause and effect which guides all forms in a proper sequence. This law applies in the conditional universe in which we all find ourselves.

According to the previous chapter on the divine Mother, nature or *prakriti* is that which is responsible for clothing the forms with their respective sheaths or *kosas*. We have different bodies in order to exist as an independent entity. The first *kosa* is *ananda-may-kosa* or "bliss sheath." This is the beginning in the process of involution or separation and the state where we mistakenly see ourselves as an independent being.

In our gradual descent into more dense realities we take on another *kosa* called the *jnana-maya-kosa* or wisdom sheath. This is a stage where we have conscious intelligence; however, we still retain or reflect the wisdom sheath. It is in the next stage we develop desire for attachments and this sheath is called *mana-maya-kosa*. *Maya* is a term which describes the veiling power of the divine mother aspect and creates the illusion of a separate existence. *Mana-maya-kosa* is the mental sheath.

Now that we have lost our pure bliss state, we start seeking enjoyments in the phenomenal or conditioned world. We have all become prodigals at this stage. The mental sheath from the effect of *prakriti* has now created mental constructs to fulfil the purpose of attaining desires. As *prakriti* proceeds to the next stage, it descends into the subtle elements and creates the *prana-maya-kosa* or energy sheath. In the last stage, it descends into the gross material world with the *anna-maya-kosa* or dense body.

Everything *prakriti* does is done according to *karmic* law. No sequence can be bypassed and so involution is complete. The stage of evolution proceeds likewise according to the law of *karma*. In the finite world of cause and effect we all are affected by the *kalchakra* or wheel of time. In Indian cosmology, time is measured on a cosmic scale by *yugas*. Beyond *prakriti* (nature) and beyond time there is oneness. We all are waves in the great ocean of spirit. It is the perturbations in the realm of *prakriti* which create the "waves", so to speak.

Each soul, as it individualises, creates its own destiny according to the peregrinations of the mind. Due to attachments in the phenomenal world it is responsible for its creations. We have finally completed the process of involution and are now on the upward path of evolution. As the *Kali Yuga* winds down, we are entering the *Dwapara Yuga* or Copper Age. We are moving away from the strictly gross manifestations of *prakriti* or nature and are entering the beginning of the more subtle manifestations. This is evident in the appearance of electricity, electronics, etc. The subtle electricities are called *sukshmabuthas*. Even our physical bodies are becoming more infused with the subtle energies.

The inexorable law of *karma* tethers one to cause and effect, and no one can escape the fruits of one's actions until the law is satisfied. *Karma yoga* is the surrendering of the fruits of action so that the Lord is seen as the doer and not the separated self. If, however, there is true repentance, then sins can be erased as there is no *karma* in Christ.

Karma can be appeased by applying a higher law whereby one's debt, even murder, can be forgiven. If in the course of true repentance and self-sacrifice one risks one's life to save another, the law of love supersedes and a previous taking of a life is eradicated as a *karmic* debt. Edgar Cayce reminded us that every day we are meeting our Self. The past catches up with the present, and we must face the consequence of our previous acts. How do we meet each situation we find ourselves immersed in? How does an adept or master act in each situation? This is the question we should ask.

> *The birth of a man is the birth of his sorrow, the longer he lives the more stupid he becomes, because the anxiety to avoid unavoidable death becomes more and more acute. What bitterness! He lives for what is always out of reach. His thirst for survival in the future makes him incapable of living in the present.*
>
> CHUANG TZU

Anxiety is increasing in modern life. Little time is spent in contemplation, meditation and spiritual practice. How then, at the moment of death, can one focus the attention on the spiritual light when the mind has never been trained? *Karma* is in the mind. Watch your thoughts. Just as seeds sprout into a giant bush or tree, so do our *samskaras*, or past tendencies, come forth to manifest. Negative thoughts and patterns must be cut at the root and not be allowed to flourish. Negative thoughts are the root cause of all ugliness in humanity: they must be replaced with positive thinking.

1) Let negative thoughts die by attrition. Do not focus your attention on them.
2) Learn the art of dynamic substitution. Replace negative thoughts with elevating thoughts.
3) Do not let your mind become empty; an idle mind is not conducive to constructive living.
4) Train your subconscious daily with prayer, meditation, and positive suggestion.

5) As negative thoughts arise, do not struggle or fight them. Agitation of the mind disturbs peace. Watch the negative dark clouds pass and be detached from them.
6) Live life simply, do not increase desires, and be moderate in all things.
7) Study the sacred scriptures of the world. A good one to start with is the *Yoga Sutras* of Patanjali. This great sage will educate you on spiritual practice.
8) Do good, see good and act through goodness. This will bring the more positive *karma* into your life.
9) "Start slowly, drive safely and arrive early."—Sai Baba.
10) Watch the conversation you have with yourself; it is the most important conversation you will ever have. Affirm only that which lifts you up.
11) Love yourself.

> *Know God, and all fetters will be loosened. Ignorance will vanish. Birth, death and rebirth will be no more. Meditate upon Him and transcend physical consciousness. Thus will you reach union with the Lord of the universe. Thus will you become identified with him who is One without a second. In Him all your desires will find fulfillment.*
>
> **SHVETASHVATARA UPANISHAD**

During any kind of *sadhana* or spiritual practice, whether it be yoga, meditation, prayer or service to mankind, dedicate all your actions to the One without a second (God) and you will be free even while alive in the body—a *Jivamukta*.

> *According as one acts, according as one conducts himself so does he become. The doer of good becomes good. The doer of evil becomes evil. One becomes virtuous by virtuous action, bad by bad action.*
>
> **BRIHADARANYAKA UPANISHAD**

THE LAW OF ONE

All of the scriptures of the world attest to the One God. Hinduism has many aspects of the One God and is mistakenly seen as polytheism. The Law of One has been around for a long time. Edgar Cayce, in his readings, spoke of the Law of One in Atlantis. In the Atlantean land, there were those who believed in the Law of One and those who followed the Sons of Belial into rebellion. Socrates, the Greek philosopher, along with Plato and Aristotle, in the mystery schools, were educated about the Monad. Leibnitz, the German thinker, also spoke of the Monad. The Law of One is inscribed in the Enneads, the Shema, Zoroastrianism, Advaita Vedanta and many other world teachings.

Mathematically, everything proceeds from no-thing or zero to One thing. In the law of Three in the succeeding chapter, we will see how the One becomes three, etc. First, there is the void or nothing. The Kabballah calls this *Ain Sof*. The beginning of manifestation is the fiery point within the circumference of the zero or no-thing. This point or *bindu* as described in the earlier chapter is the manifestation of the One or the Monad as it is sometimes called. The One represents unity before duality has occurred. In Atlantis, the Law of One was used in religion and science. The fiery point at the apex of the crystal capstone is where the cosmic forces gathered into one point of concentrated power. Oneness is a law and can be seen in nature. All the colours blend into white light.

The body of Christ is seen as One body. The Adam Kadmon (Judaism) is also one body. In the doctrine of hylozoism, everything is seen as existing in the body of a greater being. Whether microcosmic or macrocosmic, the centre of life is the monadic point in the centre. A theosophical definition of God is described as a circumference existing everywhere and centred nowhere. However, for all units of God, i.e., all monads, the circumference is around the fiery point within the centre.

The one at the centre is a dynamic vibrating point from which proceeds that creation or creature. Reduce each and every one of us and that is what remains: the ultimate atom of existence which is immortal and indestructible. All life is one: life proceeds from the one and returns back to the one. Each atom is a sun and the *Gayatri* prayer (the oldest prayer in the world) expresses this idea greater than can be explained by any other idea (See page 31 for the prayer).

On the involuntary arc the monad descends from the highest plane (seventh), all the way down to the dense physical mineral kingdom and on the evolutionary arc ascends up through the succeeding kingdoms: plant, animal, human, etc. The tabulation can be seen as follows:

Spirit	Matter
7	1
6	2
5	3
4	4
3	5
2	6
1	7

This descent and ascent of entities, in theosophical terms, are called rounds. Every planet we see in the sky has seven polarities corresponding to the respective plane of matter. Likewise, the monad in its journey travels from spirit to matter and back to spirit. This fact is revealed by the recently deployed Hubbell telescope which discovered that most of the matter in the universe is invisible. Our physical senses only relate to us the range and frequency of the plane in which we reside.

This world in which we live, our earth, according to old Brahmanical tables, has a lifecycle of approximately eight billion years. It too will reincarnate according to *karmic* law. All life proceeds from the one (monad) going through its respective cycles. The sun will eventually fulfil its cosmic life and the new sun will take birth. Everything is flashing on and flashing off.

All life has a period of cyclic existence from the point of manifestation when flashing forth and flashing off during *pralaya* (out of manifestation). A sub-atomic particle such as a tachyon may flash on for a trillionth of a second and flash out of manifestation. Stars and galaxies flash on for aeons, yet, they too much eventually flash off. Always, every particle of manifestation remains within the *One*. Each monadic existence is assigned its particular orbit within the One.

In Atlantis, initiates of the Law of One would operate according to this universal principle. The master would gather his 12 disciples and meet in the inner planes and they would all be of one mind. This can be seen in the heliocentric model used in astrology. The circle is divided into 12 with the monad or sun at the centre. We incarnate clockwise around the zodiacal wheel, the wheel of *samsara* (illusion), until we work off our *karma*. When we decide to complete the cycle of manifestation, we reincarnate counterclockwise, unite our subconscious aspects with our superconscious (monad) and make the Ascension into a higher dimension.

In the next chapter, we will see how the One divides into three: known as the Law of Three.

THE LAW OF THREE

God is imminent and transcendent; that is, He is in the manifest creation as well as beyond it. God in manifestation is Christ. In the beginning was the Word, the *Pranava (Aum)* and everything was created through sound and light. The *bindu* (point) of manifestation is the one at the centre. The fiery point vibrates and divides into two poles or masculine and feminine potencies. The relationship between these two poles produces a third aspect.

The One becoming the many is an on-rolling process in the universe where the One undivided *Atman*, a huge organism in which the inmost nucleus and pervading spirit and Self is the one abiding being. The one supreme person, *Purusha*, in his aspect as *Brahman*, the Word as *Isha,* the Lord, who decrees that every moving thing—and all things are moving—in this universe of constant flux yet shall and will move in ranges or orbits which are assigned to them; however, the ranges and limits can be so widened as to be coextensive with the whole. Every part and particle is entified or ensouled by the all-pervasive, all-feeling *Atman*. This on-rolling process where the One becomes the many is called *vivarta*.

In Western concepts such as hylozoism, everything exists in the body of a greater being—cells exist in you, you exist within humanity, humanity exists within the world, the world exists within the solar system, suns within constellations, etc. The Laws of One, Three and Seven are fundamental to all entities within the whole.

In the uncanonical scripture, the Apocrypha, it says, split a stone in half and I am there. There exists the being of life in every single atom, electron, sub-atomic particle, in every *anu* or *parananu*. Not only does He exist in part or in fragment but in his full undivided being.

In no other scripture but the *Vedas* did the Vedic seers perceive this unvarnished truth. There is the story about Prahlada, a boy in the demon race who was tortured by his wicked father, and he appealed to the Divine to rescue him, who got a response from a stone pillar. The Divine Being, in response to Prahlada's burning love for Him, arose from the pillar to save him. These Vedic seers perceived that behind every part of the phenomenon of nature, visible and invisible, exists a *deva* or shining one which flashed forth from the One. Incorrectly did the Hindus interpret these *devas* (angels) as personification of nature (gods); whereas, the correct interpretation would be the very spirit of and Self of the universe seen through Nature's forms as through a prism.

> *TRUTH IS WITHIN OURSELVES, IT TAKES NO RISE*
> *From outward things, whate'ver you may believe*
> *There is an inmost centre in us all,*
> *Where truth abides in fullness; and around.*
>   **ROBERT BROWNING**

The prism first divides into three and then into seven as in the Law of Seven. The mathematical formula for this is $2^{x-1} = pc$. Two to the x-power minus one equals all possible combinations. Substituting the Law of Three, using 3 for x, the formula $2^{3-1} = 7$. The One becomes three, and then 7.

As the one divides into its opposite pole, there is always a third factor involved as the following tabulation illustrates.

male	androgyne	female
day	dusk	night
proton	neutron	electron
spirit	soul	matter
thesis	synthesis	antithesis
vertical	hypotenuse	base
father	son	mother
transparent	translucent	opaque
positive	neutral	negative
past	present	future

The Law of Three teaches that for every polar opposite there is a mediating principle at the centre. In the Tao, the constant interchange between the two furies produces the whole universe as it appears in a constant state of flux, but forever remains the Tao or the whole. The white light as it enters the prism divides into three primary colours, and following the combination of the primary colours the light divides into the spectrum of seven colours. When you as a monad or spirit enter a physical body, the interplay of your God-spark with the material world creates your soul. The soul is your God-spark in manifestation. Christ is God in manifestation. The person in manifestation is a unit of seven; that is, a divine spark (monad) connected to all seven planes of manifestation through seven *chakras*. As you leave the planes of manifestation on your return back to the One (Monad), you return with all of your experiences.

The one undivided idea becomes the idol or facsimile of the idea. The idea is invisible and the idol is visible. The ideal is the meditating principle between them both as exhibited in the Law of Three. God, the invisible, is the light of mind as Walter Russell illustrates in his teachings (See *A New Concept of the Universe* by Walter Russell). God is all-knowing in his universal mind of his One idea. In Him is absolute balance and stillness. He is in a state of complete rest. He has no motion, no form, does not change, is stillness and is no-thing or zero. Yet, in this zero state is the absolute reality. The reality of matter in which we find ourselves is a simulated one which is divided by his centring idea into extended poles of his thinking. It is the zero condition which is eternal and absolute containing the extended poles of his thinking.

The life-death cycle is merely two halves of a whole. The giving and regiving, the enfolding and the refolding process is eternal in the one idea. Jesus said that no one could take his life but that he could lay it down and take it up again. This is being at one mind with the Creator. I am the alpha and the omega or the beginning and the end. There is no time and space in the zero point as there is no beginning or end. (See the chapter on Eternity, Chapter 2).

The triune of spirit, soul and body illustrates the Law of Three. The first three *chakras* form the upper triad of your sevenfold energy system. The *bindu* point (father) is the top of the head or fontanelle. The third eye (Christ centre) or *ajna chakra* is the son. The Holy Spirit is the medulla area behind the head. The over-self works through the master gland in the head and the Christ pattern (ideal) sets the pattern which the personality must follow:

"Behold, I stand at the door and knock..."

The individual personality must open the door to the Christ-self. The other glands represented by the four beasts: eagle, lion, man and calf, respectively, correspond to the four elements air, fire, water and earth. The four beasts must give homage to Him who sits on the throne (over-self).

All of the trinitarian religions attest to this threefold division of man and God. The Huna religion calls the over-self the *Aumakua* or divine parental spirit. The Law of Three as formulated in the equation $2^{x-1} = pc$ is a universal model based on the binary system used in computers today. Einstein said that God does not throw dice with the universe and that there is an orderly sequence to things whether we perceive it or not. Emerson speaks of the One thus:

The Supreme Critic on the errors of the past and the present and the only prophet of that which must be, is that great nature in which we rest as the earth lies in the soft arms of the atmosphere; that Unity, that Over-Soul, within which every man's particular being is contained and made one with all other, that common heart of which all sincere conversation is the worship, to which all right action is submission; that overpowering reality which confutes our tricks and talents, and constrains everyone to pass for what he is, and to speak from his character and not from his tongue, and which evermore tends to pass into our thought and hand and becomes wisdom and virtue and power and beauty. We live in succession, in division, in parts, in particles. Meantime, within man is the soul of the whole; the wise silence, the universal beauty, to which every part and particle is equally related; the eternal One. And this deep power in which we exist and whose beautitude is all accessible to us, is not only self-sufficing and perfect in every hour, but the act of seeing and the things seen, the seer and the spectacle, the subject and the object, are one.

RALPH WALDO EMERSON, THE OVER-SOUL

THE LAW OF SEVEN

> *PHILOSOPHY WILL CLIP AN ANGEL'S WINGS,*
> *Conquer all mysteries by rule and line.*
> *Empty the haunted air, the gnomed mine,*
> *Unweave a rainbow.*
>
> **JOHN KEATS, LAMIA**

Let us unweave the sevenfold coloured rainbow as we look into the Law of Seven. It took seven years to build the temple, as seven days of creation. Thousands of workers: energies, atoms, the laws of life. The physical temple represents the physical universe. The creative triad, under the Law of Three, represented elsewhere by the threefold god of India, Shiva shows that all energy manifests through triads. These finally build up the soul temple through interaction of creative energies, as life gradually matured and brought to ripening.

Each people has given a different explanation in the tenets of their religions of the number seven. It was the number of numbers for those initiated into the ancient mysteries. It is the vehicle of life containing body and soul, since it is formed of a quarternary and of a trinity. Let us touch upon the initiation into sacred mysteries respecting the seven-rayed god, lighting up every soul.

The rainbow is a bridge between the unreal and the real, the invisible to the visible, as well as doorway that leads to the mysteries, imagination and fairy tales. In the Old Testament, it is the symbol of the Covenant between man and God. The immortal laws of God extend to the mortal realm of man. God's law is not a law of compulsion but a law of harmony and rhythm. Science has revealed to us that the colours of the rainbow are not just a hallucination of the human brain, but actually are the visible representation or emanation of all the elements which go to make up matter itself.

Not only do the colours of the rainbow reflect the spectrum of the physical world, but colours have their respective spiritual activity as well. Joseph's coat of many colours, the auras and halo of saints and the electromagnetic nature of the human auras depict the streams of life-force and spiritual power pouring in and through all living things.

Edgar Cayce relates colours, notes and planets as follows:

Red	Do	Mars
Orange	Re	Sun
Yellow	Mi	Mercury
Green	Fa	Saturn
Blue	Sol	Jupiter
Indigo	La	Venus
Violet	Ti	Moon

Spiritual or occult science teaches that the Great Central Sun emanates these great vibratory rays or a wavelength of light, forming the seven basic main types of human characteristics.

1. Violet—Spiritual power
2. Indigo—Intuition
3. Blue—Inspiration
4. Green—Energy (supply)
5. Yellow—Wisdom
6. Orange—Health
7. Red—Life

The Great Pyramid symbolised the number seven—the combination of three and four, or the triangle on a square base. There are only two basic forms in the universe, the cube (mother) and the sphere (father). These two forces which extend to the cube of space (centrifugal and centripetal) to form incandescent suns form the basis for the optical universe. The *bindu* point at the top of the pyramid is the centre where these two forces meet. The two interlocking triads in the Star of David with the *bindu* or point in the centre also illustrate this.

In man these two forces are outgoing toward the senses centrifugally or inward toward the soul centripetally. In meditation, the senses are shut down and the spiritual forces (*kundalini*) rise up the spine to meet the soul. The Law of Seven is basic to the understanding of the universe.

The Law of Seven derives from the three rays of aspect which form the four rays of attribute. In the formula $2^{x-1} = pc$, substituting 3 for x, the combination = seven. Another way of illustrating this is:

> Let A = Father
> Let B = Son
> Let C = Holy Spirit

ABC	None predominates
ABC	A predominates
ABC	B predominates
ABC	C predominates
ABC	BC predominate
ABC	AB predominate
ABC	All three predominate

This binary system of base 10 can be used to describe the seven rays:

1. Will and power
2. Love and wisdom
3. Active intelligence
4. Harmony through conflict
5. Concrete science and knowledge
6. Devotion
7. Ceremonial order and magic

The fourth ray is the mediating principle between the first three rays of aspect and the last three rays of attribute. Rays five, six and seven represent truth, goodness and beauty. These cosmic intelligences (rays) are known by various other names: the seven Sephira, the seven spirits before the throne, the seven Elohim, etc. Due to periodicity of the different astrological ages, every 2000 years, a different ray comes into prominence. The last 2000 years was marked by the sixth ray of devotion. Lord Jesus, the Piscean avatar, so enfired humanity with his love and devotion to the father, the world has not been the same. Each astrological age is also characterised by the reflexive sign. Virgo is the polar opposite to Pisces on the zodiacal wheel; hence, Mary the Virgin devotionally leads us to her son who then takes us to the father.

The seventh ray of Ceremonial Order and Magic will characterise the incoming Aquarian Age. The first ray is the ray of synthesis on a primary level; that is, Shiva contains both Vishnu and Brahma. The seventh ray is the ray which synthesises all the rays and is the lowest densification of the light. It relates the invisible to the visible, the unseen to the seen, hence, the ray of magic.

The early Greeks looked for harmony, order and synthesis in the world. They called the world *Kosmos* and Pythagoras sought out harmony, proportion and geometrical perfection. Music was the Pythagorean model for harmony and perfection but was only one model for the *Kosmos*. He also knew a great deal about astronomy. Anaximander, who was younger than Thales but older than Pythagoras, postulated that up and down had no meaning in the *Kosmos*. He said the universe was a great fluid vortex and the sun and moon were circular vortexes of rotating fire. The sun, he said, was an opening like a nozzle in a pair of bellows. Pythagoras himself believed the earth to be freely suspended in space. It was Parmenides from Elea, a new Greek colony in southern Italy, who later correctly taught that the earth was spherical and the moon reflected light. These early thinkers were constantly looking for order and synthesis in the *Kosmos*, and now the seventh ray of order and synthesis is upon us in this dawning of the Aquarian Age.

What will this order and synthesis be? Already, great geometrical designs are appearing in crop circles all over the world or *Kosmos*. The higher intelligence has already decreed that order and synthesis will come about. Look at the intricate design in computer chips today. The higher intelligence is also visiting us from various civilisations and other dimensions to reveal to us an even larger order and synthesis. This is not only the end of a 2000-year cycle, but the end of a 26,000-year cycle as well. The end has come, but also a new beginning.

TWILIGHT OF THE GODS

> *All appearances are verily one's own concepts self-conceived in the mind, like reflections seen in the mirror.*
>
> **PADMA SAMBHAVA**

In the Aquarian Age, as man comes into maturity, through rapid mental development, he must face his own creations (concepts) and this, my friend, is a fearful thing. Individually and collectively, man must face the "dweller on the threshold" before he can unfold true soul culture. We are now positioned in evolution to fight the battle of Armageddon of the mind. In this battle, man will come face to face with the anti-Christ which Anthroposophist, Rudolf Steiner, calls Ahriman.

Edgar Cayce taught that there were 17 incarnations of Jesus in which he taught monotheism. In one of those lives he was the prophet Zoroaster. Zoroaster taught of the ancient battle between Ahriman, the lord of darkness and Ahura Mazda, the solar logos or the lord of light. Intelligence without love is dangerous and this is the current lesson that man will face under Ahriman. Christ is love-wisdom. The intelligence in the mind must be fused with love in the heart. There will come a time when man's natural love will grow cold. Technology will not be the saviour of man if it leads to his utter destruction. Whom will you serve?

Cayce, speaking in 1942 about the dangers in the world, said, "Yes, for there will be the breaking up until the time when there are people in every land who will say that this or that shows the hand of divine interference—or that nature is taking a hand—or that this or that is the natural consequence of good judgement... let each declare whom ye will serve: a man, a state, or thy God." The shifting of the poles in the year A.D. 2000 to 2001 is predicted, and this will inaugurate the beginning of a new cycle.

Using the heliocentric model of the solar system, with the Sun at the centre, during May 2000, the Sun, Mercury, Venus, Mars, Jupiter and Saturn will be in the sign Taurus. In this model, the earth is in the opposing sign of Scorpio facing all that pull from the 180-degree opposition. Could this be the pole shift and telluric changes that Cayce and other prophets foresaw?

It is the anti-Christ forces which have been allowed to permeate our culture with the materialistic concepts that there is no life after death and that everything can be explained in a materialistic, scientific fashion. We are not a completed being until we return to the spiritual realms. We are gods in the making and evolution is a crossroad whereby we must use our talents and have to give an account for the right-useness or mis-useness of them. The moral imperative is greater now than it has ever been. The seventh ray will bring an intensification of light and darkness and choices will have to be made.

According to Steiner, humanity has already lived through the birth of Lucifer and Christ into the world and now awaits the arrival of Ahriman. Lucifer represents the past and would have us live there. Ahriman would like to take us into the future. Both want to take us away from the present. While in a human body we are subject to time, whereas, in the realm and dimension of our spirit there is no such thing. Edgar Cayce informs us that there is no time and space to our spiritual self. Carl Jung asserts likewise:

> *I simply believe that some part of the human Self or soul is not subject to the laws of space and time.*
> CARL GUSTAV JUNG

The conscious mind is only a fragment of our being. Cayce informs us that when we die, our conscious mind recedes into our subconscious and remains in the repository of our soul memory. In Zen teachings, as well as Cayce's, the goal is to unite the conscious mind with the subconscious and go into the superconsciousness. Eastern teachings call this the *Turiya* state.

Along with earth changes in the new age to come, there may be dimensional changes as well. We may develop new organs of perception and consciousness may evolve out of time into the state of the eternal now. The motto for Aquarius is "I know." Science comes from the Latin *sciere*, "to know". The knowledge of science is empirically based and is in the realm and dimension of the senses. Ahriman will try to keep us sense bound. Lucifer is the glory and knowledge of the past; Ahriman is the knowledge of the future. *Brahman* is forever now, the whole universe is recreated every moment in the *Now*.

Knowing is in the present moment; knowledge goes on forever, it is not knowing. Knowledge concerns the past and the future. The Tao is a river-like flow of knowing in the moment, every moment. When asked to describe it, the moment is past and it becomes knowledge to be placed in the archives, in a book, and is not alive. The knowers, Lao Tse, Mahavir, Buddha. Christ, Sai Baba, etc. are in constant *samadhi* and exist simultaneously in all dimensions, in all places and in all time because they are not fragmented into separated selves.

Science wants to divide everything into its components, control all variables and deal with constants. Aristotle reminds us that the only thing that is constant is change. It would do well for the scientists to remind themselves that the universe is created through sound and light. Examination of the physical universe through the senses is like trying to describe an elephant by looking only at the tip of his trunk.

> *By getting to smaller and smaller units, we do not come to fundamental units, or indivisible units, but we do come to a point where division has no meaning.*
>
> **WERNER HEISENBERG**

The illusion is created by the three *gunas: Sattva, Rajas* and *Tamas*. The opaqueness of matter is caused by the *Tamasic guna*, activity is caused by the *Rajasic guna* and the *Sattva guna* balances the two. Only in the one undivided Self does fragmentation occur. The problem with knowing *Brahman* comes in being an observer, a separated self or fragment; hence, the dilemma of having an ego. *Brahman* can never really be known as a thing of science. The *Upanishads* make this clear. God is not a thing or, rather, He is no-thing. He is a process, a continuum, a flow like the Tao which cannot be captured and stored away.

This Mysterium is a mystery because it can never be known; as that which is always new, eternal, etc., cannot be codified, placed in a scripture, tucked away and solved. How can you finish the eternal or relegate it to the past or the future?

> *The truth is that you are always united with the Lord. But you must know this. Nothing further is there to know. Meditate, and you will realise that mind, matter, and Maya [the power which unites mind and matter] are but three aspects of* Brahman, *the one reality.*
>
> *Fire, though present in the fire sticks, is not perceived until one stick is rubbed against another. The Self is like that fire: it is realised in the body by meditation of the sacred syllable OM...*

> *Like oil in seasame seeds, butter in cream, water in the river bed, fire in tinder, the Self dwells within the Soul. Realise Him through truthfulness and meditation.*
>
> *Like butter in cream is the Self in everything. Knowledge of the Self is gained through meditation. The Self is* Brahman. *By* Brahman *is all ignorance 'destroyed'.*
>
> **SHVETASHVATARA UPANISHAD**

First we must realise our ignorance in the face of the unknowable, leave the past behind, do not worry about the future and rest in the arms of the divine. If past is prologue, then why be concerned about repetition? The twilight of the gods rests in the eternal now, whether it be a cosmic day, a solar year, a nanosecond or some bygone history. There is only one Self, one now and one reality.

> ### One
>
> *We have one world to live in*
> *One sphere in which to die*
> *One ray of hope to cling to*
> *One heart to satisfy*
>
> *One faith in which to worship*
> *One truth to call our own*
> *One path in which to follow*
> *One peaceful temperate zone*
>
> *One clarion call to answer*
> *One deity which we call God*
> *One single borrowed moment*
> *One fertile earthen sod*
>
> *One abyss in which to plummet*
> *One heaven to rise above*
> *Yet, the greatest need for man*
> *Remains—One true and lasting love.*
>
> **SAI GRAFIO**

DREAMS
THE FABRIC OF THE UNIVERSE

The Western concepts of dreams are not given the same weight as the Indian text. Illusion, transience, falsity and cognisance of the ephemeral nature of dreams in the West are antithetical to Indian concepts. In the West, the waking state is considered substantial and the Indian sees only *maya* (illusion) in the waking state. Since the waking state is a distorted image of the Godhead, it is considered unreal (illusory) by Indian standards. This science was lain down in the *Upanishads* (c. 700 B.C.)

These texts describe four states: waking, dreaming, dreamless sleep and the fourth supernatural state called *Turiya*. In the waking state one knows consensus reality or that which is common to others. In the dream state we know what is private to us in our inner world. In the third state of dreamless sleep the dreamer creates and destroys the whole world which is a common theme in Indian scriptures. If we can understand that we are dreaming when we think we are awake, then we can move toward enlightenment or the fourth state. This fourth state is the first three in totality. This is why Indian philosophy considers the world as *maya*.

Once again, from the Indian point of view, waking and dreaming are both *cul-de-sacs* of reality. Our basic condition is that of illusion. We have built up over many lives *vasanas* or tendencies due to our variegated desires. One might say that our mind is just a bundle of these desires. We pride ourselves in the waking state with our rational mind to be vigilant and resistant to illusion or falsity; however, when we are asleep we do not question all the various experiences which might seem preposterous. We then wake up and try to correlate these dreams with our waking life to make some sense out of them. What we have for reality is merely a collection of assumptions. We tend to think in terms of metaphors or similes, comparing one thing to another in the ever-expanding world of assumptions only to have them transform into something else; until we get to *Brahman*, the unknowable, for there is nothing in which to compare.

The answer lies in the mind which eventually has to be destroyed. The mind is merely a bundle of desires which can be easily agitated. He who has control of the mind, *chitta*, or consciousness, can realise the *atman* which is part of the *paramatman*. The Self is above pleasure and pain, joy or sorrow, riches and poverty. The dream bubbles are the same as water and so are the multiplicity of all names and forms. All water from the rivers must flow into the sea, so too must all transient desires lose themselves in the all blissful realised soul.

The world or *Jagath* is none other than the outpicturing of the mind which exists in the waking state. You say that "I have seen it with my very eyes." Behind those eyes is your mind with all its tendencies coloured by your own unique experiences. *Sathya* is truth. The first act of warfare is deception. There is constant warfare going on between earth and heaven, between the seen and the unseen. In Emphesians we are told to put on our full armour, the sword (truth), the helmet and the breastplate. Paul says that we do not wrestle with flesh and blood. We see through a glass darkly and have many veils of illusion surrounding us. Now, the lines are drawn and heaven and earth are coming together due to the influence of the seventh ray. Darkness is being squeezed out and there will be nowhere to hide. Where were we hiding in the first place, since everything is known? We have been hiding from ourselves—our true Self.

The dream or illusion is really the ego (*ahamkara*) or the separated self. The left side of our body is the feminine or unconscious self. The right side is the conscious or masculine self. We as conscious beings stand outside the totality of our being and are in need of salvation. We are redeemed when we integrate the lost side of our nature. Isaiah prophesied the mystery between the despised person and the saviour:

> *A thing despised and rejected by men,*
> *a man of sorrows and familiar with suffering,*
> *a man to make people screen their faces;*
> *He was despised and we took no account of him.*
> **ISAIAH 53:3**

When the lost part of ourself is saved, then we are brought into the kingdom. The ego has to be removed and the lost part (unconscious self) has to be included so as to connect us with our soul. Allegorically, the story of the good Samaritan, the despised one who stoops down to rescue us; so, paradoxically it is the inner beggar who ends up as the redeemer.

From the point of view of *maya* or illusion, demons, ghosts, ghouls and goblins represent the unintegrated elements of the universe or that which is hidden from the light. *Asurya*, etymologically in Sanskrit, denotes "a" (without), and *surya* (light). These demons represent the madness and hubris of the full-blown ego.

Everything, essentially, is divine, including matter, as God is in all; however, spirit is matter when cognised by the pellucid senses. The world is not impure because the impurities reside within us. You feel you are the senses only so you are drowned in misery. The five senses are all bound up with the mind: the mind it is that separately activates the senses and is affected by their reactions. Man reads through the mind associated eye and so he fails. One has to see with the divine eye. *Maya* flourishes in ignorance and absence of discrimination. The world is an illusion which, on account of the play of *maya*, seems to be subject to evolution of names and forms and involution of the same until the whole thing is extinguished in the *pralaya* (return) of the cosmic breath.

The eloquent Shakespeare, in these famous lines, has captured the dreamlike quality as the fabric of the universe:

> ...*These our actors,*
> *As I foretold you, were all spirits, and*
> *Are melted into air, into thin air;*
> *And, like the baseless fabric of this vision,*
> *The cloud-capped towers, the gorgeous palaces,*
> *The solemn temples, the great globe itself,*
> *Yes, all that which is inherent, shall dissolve,*
> *And, like this insubstantial pageant faded,*
> *Leave not a rack behind. We are such stuff*
> *As dreams are made on, and our little life*
> *Is rounded with a sleep.*

MAGIC OF THE
SEVENTH ORDER

As stated in the previous chapters, the corporeal ego falsely believes in the illusory duality of itself and the physical world. In order to maintain this illusion, it expends a great deal of automaton energy in the constant maintenance of the world and the ego. Magic is merely removing this automaton energy, thus, destroying the illusion and freeing up the energy to be redirected toward the celestial realms. Notwithstanding the ephemeral nature of matter, that is, forms are changing, decaying and being reborn, the ego still maintains itself as a separate independent existence.

Who we are is of celestial origin; sons and daughters of light, or divine rays from those spheres. The divine ray passes from the Divine sphere to the celestial, to the constellations, to the sun, planets and finally to the moon. Now, in the Hermetic doctrines—*The Poimandres*—there (the moon) we entered into generation. We saw our image in the water and fell in love with it. It was here in the irrational sphere, where we merged into matter and became half divine and half beast. The Cayce readings are replete with stories of how the celestial sons got caught up in their own creations.

Magic is merely dropping the automaton energy, recognising the ever-changing world of nature and redirecting the energy from the horizontal to the vertical or celestial realms. Animal spines are horizontal or parallel to the earth,

operating under the lunar forces, whereas, man's spine is
erect and is directed toward the celestial or solar spheres. The
magician, while dropping the illusory ego in the world effects
and changing phenomena, rises to the level of causation and
can thereby effect changes. A miracle is from the invisible to
the visible, from the unseen to the seen or vice versa. Now,
this is the Magic of the Seventh Order as the seventh ray
ingress with the Aquarian Age.

The seventh ray is the ray of Ceremonial Order and
Magic which is wholly tied in with ritual. The significance of
ritual is that everything has meaning. There is meaning in
everything which portends; auguries, omens, signs and
wonders. We are a microcosm which is a mirror image of the
microcosm. In the *nous* there is only the divine mind of
eternal images as in Plato's *Timaeus*. That which is here in
the world has its reflection in the eternal realm of divine ideas.
Ritual and ceremony are the active forms of the divine, the
intermediate (psychic realm) and the material world
simultaneously. The true magician has access to all worlds—
physical, emotional, mental and nouemenal; or, earth, water,
fire and etheric. In the Tibetan *Stupta* these elements are
arranged in ascending order. ·

Zen, which deals with the here and now or Buddha
nature, is very much tied in with ritual. The Japanese tea
ceremony is very seventh ray. Doing everything precisely in
the same manner at the same time, like taking your shoes off
before entering a sanctuary, lighting candles and incense,
etc., is all very seventh ray. *Mudras*, or hand gestures, are
also rituals and are symbolic of inner and outer realities. The
most common *mudra* is the touching of the forefinger with
the thumb, a common *mudra* used in Tibetan meditations.
This signifies the individualised *jiva* (soul) linking up with the
over-soul or *paramatman*.

In most rituals and forms of magic, the law of invocation
and evocation is employed. The invocation is the asking and
the evocation is the response or the answer. Most prayers are
invocations like the Lord's Prayer. The mistake most people

make when they pray or meditate is that they ask, but do not
sit quietly and patiently for a response. The soul is feminine
and has to take its request to the father (masculine), and it is
incumbent upon the soul to wait for the answer.

Correspondence is another law upon which magic is
based. Paracelsus came up with the doctrine of signatures as
to the use of stones, plants, stars, etc. The sunflower
corresponds to the sun, elemental iron to the planet Mars,
moonstone to the moon, and infinitum. Knowing these
correspondences, a herbalist can use certain plants for
healing. This simple unity between man and the cosmos,
albeit overstretched, cannot be denied. Yellow plants,
resembling yellow jaundice, are used to treat liver ailments.
Poultices used to treat the wounds of the human body can be
obtained from pith which is obtained from the wounds of
trees.

This law of correspondence goes much deeper as to the
relation of planetary and stellar influences to human destiny.
The precise juxtaposition of the stars at the moment of birth
is a crystallised map of human destiny. There are many views
on this subject, however, varying from predeterminism to
free will.

> *It is not in the stars that we are underlings but
> rather in ourselves.*
>
> **SHAKESPEARE**

Yet, at the same time he espouses a different view:

> *There is a destiny which guides us, rough hew it as
> we will, there is a destiny which carves our ends*
>
> **WILLIAM SHAKESPEARE**

From one point of view, the horizontal one, man's
destiny is indelibly fixed and preordained from birth as the
fixed position in his horoscope attest. Due to the merits or
lack of it from previous birth, his human ego has acquired

numerous *karmas* which have to play themselves out in the present lifetime as determined by the natal horoscope. This horizontal approach is not the one of the magician who operates from the vertical stance. The word "zodiac" from the Greek means circle of animals. Man's descent from his celestial origin is locked into the prison house of his human ego, thus circumscribed by the accretions of wants and desires or proclivities from many births. These *vasanas* or tendencies are very hard to overcome if one maintains the posture that we are indeed the ego with its inherent desires and *karmas*. The beasts of the zodiac, within us, are in darkness as they pertain to the limited stance of the human ego.

The other viewpoint of astrology is that the beast within us does not have to have dominion when we are ruled by the over-Self and have risen above lust, greed, envy and egotism. If man invokes his free will from the vertical correspondence to his soul, then he rules his fate and his destiny. If he elects that his ego govern, then the planets tug him around according to the dictates of his animal nature.

The seventh ray, being the ray of synthesis, will unite heaven and earth, male and female, consciousness and unconsciousness, the invisible with the visible, the microcosm with the macrocosm and most other polar opposites. As the light shines, it intensifies the darkness and each wrestles with the other as is seen in the increasing conflict in the world, until critical mass is reached. There is much mass in motion today; everything is speeded up on the physical level as well as the mental level. When the synthesis of mass and motion reaches critical mass, then there will be a consciousness shift as well to accommodate the change. This will be a Christ Mass for the earth itself as the planet will go through an electrification or an illumination. Magic is concerned with transformation and transmutation. *Prima materia* or the baseness of matter is elevated to its higher correspondence. Just as carbon represents the lifeless, darkness-based element in the earth, its transmutation to the clear brilliant diamond is caused by the application of heat and pressure. The pressure is on now for us to collectively align ourselves to the cosmic fire and transform our beastly nature to the diamond nature of our being.

> *Om mane padme om.*
>
> *O thou jewel within the heart of the lotus.*

SATURN
GRIM REAPER OR TEACHER

It is the goal of human evolution to attain Universal consciousness, but first man must pass the Guardian of the Threshold. That Guardian of the Threshold is Satan as described in the prologue of Job. Job is the story of Everyman and stands in for the ego which must be purified. We are all tied to the wheel of *samsara* (death and rebirth) and will remain there for aeons until the soul has worked out its *karma* and passes its test. Saturn (Satan) is the tester whereby each soul is on probation and must endure the trials and temptations as evidenced by Job. Job's career of sorrow is ultimately crowned by illumination which he achieved by passing the Guardian of the Threshold.

The ego does not want to give up its position in the life of a man and will put up a battle for ascendancy over the spiritual Self. The ego will rage this battle with opinion, rationalisation and argument until it is brought down through lessons of humility. On the exoteric plane Saturn represents the forces of contraction; on the esoteric plane as sorrow and affliction. Once the Saturnian lesson is learned, the probationary disciple passes the Guardian of the Threshold and is cognisant of a higher universal law operating spiritually behind the material plane. Saturn, ruling the sign Capricorn, is known as "The Gateway to the Gods" and Cancer, the opposite sign, is the door to involution or birth into matter.

Sorrow is the redeemer and awakener of the soul, and these trials and temptations should be used as stepping stones and not stumbling blocks. All the afflictions of the body serve to purify the soul and should be welcomed by the spiritual aspirant. Just as iron and steel are tempered and forged, so too the soul must be tried in the fire for its endurance and strength of purpose. Unselfishness must be acquired and the ego's desire for self-aggrandisement should be relinquished.

In an individual's natal chart, the placement of Saturn indicates the test and trials and purpose for which the soul chose the present incarnation to work out the *karma* and its mission on the earth plane. At the age of $28^1/_2$, Saturn returns to its original placement in the natal chart and the dance begins. Does the individual follow the proclivities, wants and desires of the Satanic ego or does it follow the path of mastery and redemption? The soul appropriates a physical vehicle upon birth, and the child learns to develop the body and masters walking, talking and growth until the age of seven. The seven-year cycles are cycles of Saturn (testing). At the age of eight, the soul appropriates an astral body through which the child learns to emote and relate to the environment through feeling. After that seven-year cycle, the mental body begins to evince itself which culminates in young adulthood. If the personality is thoroughly integrated by the Saturn return, then the soul begins to manifest by outlining the *karmic* destiny for good or ill.

No soul comes into incarnation by accident. This is the lesson of humility. Every soul has a purpose for which it has chosen to incarnate. *Karma* done correctly becomes *dharma*. *Dharma* is correct *karma*. Each individual's *dharma* is unique to that person. We cannot judge another's place in the scheme of things unless we are able to read the *akashic* records. Edgar Cayce called this record the Book of Life as described in the *Bible*. The lessons of life are distilled in the soul and become the grist for the mill.

> *The mills of the gods grind slow but they grind exceeding small and the devil (Satan) will have his due.*
>
> **Anonymous**

As the story of Job opens, he is esteemed for being wealthy and a man of influence. Isn't this what the masses of humanity aspire to? The ego is self-satisfied and sees no need for spiritual progress. He felt pious as does every hard-working person who accumulates wealth. He was stunned when the afflictions came. The ego always says "Why me?" and rails under sudden misfortune. No one is exempt from the test and trials which befall all of humanity:

- Death, the reaper, who separates us from kith and kin.
- Disease, illness and physical privation.
- Abandonment from friends and loved ones.

The Lord commended Job for his faithfulness but did not count him righteous; nevertheless, Job was willing to submit. Though Job was outwardly righteous to convention and exterior religious observance, he was not counted wise by interior spiritual standards. The mortal ego cannot function apart from the body with its attendant senses and does not have spiritual perception. It took a voice coming out of the whirlwind to reveal to him the mysteries of creation. The mysteries cannot be revealed until the interior of the human aura is illumined.

Saturn represents the mountaintop experience which every soul experiences during its long upward climb of evolution. Jesus was taken up there to be tested by Satan who promised to give him all the things of this world if he pledged obedience to him. Dr. Martin Luther King, a Capricorn, made his famous mountaintop speech attesting to his long upward climb to attain liberation. In the writings of the Tibetan Master Dwhjal Khul, written by Alice A. Bailey, the Capricorn *mantra* is revealed:

> *Lost I am in light supernal and on that light, I turn my back.*

After passing the test and trials of Saturn, the initiate, lost in the eternal light, must now turn his back and become the World Teacher. This is the positive aspect of Saturn. Religionists often speak of the wrath of God, but the trials and tribulations which visit us are more for our protection.

> *I delivered the poor that cried, and the fatherless, and him that had none to help him.*
> *The blessing of him that was ready to perish came upon me; and I caused the widow's heart to sing for joy.*
> *I put on righteousness, and it clothed me: my judgement was as a robe and a diadem.*
> *I was eyes to the blind, and feet was I to the lame.*
> *I was a father to the poor: and the cause which I searched out.*
> *And I broke the jaws of the wicked, and plucked the spoil of his teeth.*
> *Though it may not be apparent, God is with us during all the trials and vicissitudes of life.*
> **JOB 29:12-17**

Saturn represents the scaffolding of the ego, the structure which we build on the material plane. Once the structure is erected we tend to rely solely on our ego strength, not realising that there is a higher life which sustains us.

In the teachings of Gurijieff, he speaks of a cycle of seven years when the soul sends the ego conscious shocks. These shocks can come mildly to awaken the ego out of its complacency; however, if the ego chooses to ignore the lesson, then the shock becomes more severe during the succeeding seven-year cycle. At the culmination of the Saturn return, the lessons should be solidly integrated and mastered or the entire structure will collapse.

Job had succeeded in integrating his personality as he felt successful in the material world and was at a loss to understand why misfortune had befallen him. No one can remain complacent as to their spiritual progress. We are either moving forward or lagging behind. A conscious choice must be made when one reaches the mountaintop of material success; awaken to a higher reality or fall back into complacency.

The old teachings of Saturn declared that he who learns the lessons of this teacher has gained control over earth and heaven. Saturn becomes our friend admonishing to Everyman as he did Job, "Thine own hand can save thee." Saturn, the Guardian of the Threshold, will allow us passage to the heavens (*Ouranos*) when we submit ourselves as Job did, to a higher reality beyond the material ego.

THE TRANS-
SATURNIAN PLANETS
URANUS-NEPTUNE AND PLUTO

Saturn is the last outpost of the mortal ego. The Saturn constructs are pretty much in place during the first Saturn return; the personality is erected and the scaffolding removed. The dance of life after the age of 30 can include soul awareness or, like St. Paul said, "Some men grow old and die never maturing past childhood." If done properly, the integrated personality can become the soul-infused personality which eventually matures into full universal awareness.

The planets beyond Saturn bring a growing awareness of the universal order in the larger scheme of things. Whereas the mature Saturnian becomes a planetary citizen, the God-realised soul becomes the cosmic citizen. Edgar Cayce spoke of Pluto as a growing influence in the affairs of men, bringing awareness of influence beyond the confines of our immediate solar system. This influence is already upon us through UFO phenomena, crop circles, spirit channeling, etc.

Uranus is called the planet of awakening, bringing swift revolutionary change and sweeping away entirely outmoded, antiquated (Saturn) concepts. On the exoteric plane, Uranus rules electricity and the etheric; on the esoteric plane love and brotherhood. The waters in Aquarius are ethereal waters which bring a higher life.

Neptune is also a transcendental planet which can be a spiritualising influence on man if he can rise to its subtle spiritual influences. That mysterious substance which the alchemists call *Azoth*, a refined essence of spiritual power, metaphysicians say, is ruled by Neptune. Alchemy is concerned with transmutation from base metal into gold. These alchemists called the crucible in which this process took place man's spinal cord. The bony part is ruled by Saturn. The spiritualised fire which ascends up the base of the spine is the power of Neptune. When the fire reaches the top of the head which houses the master glands, then the higher awakening takes place.

These outer planets are not fully understood yet as man's spiritual development has not reached the goal of higher attainment. On the physical plane, Neptune can represent deception, fraud, lying, weakness and is felt mostly, in a negative sense, through imbibing alcohol and drugs. Its vibration is like the most sensitive string on a harp; striking the highest spiritual note or getting easily out of tune. Neptune can cloud perception and cause one to get lost in the world of *maya* (illusion).

The planet Pluto brings upheaval, revolution and cataclysms. In its highest sense, it is Shiva or the destroyer of forms. At the end of every age this Shiva aspect comes into prominence and brings the transforming changes as foretold by Edgar Cayce and Nostradamus in the coming earth changes. It is the lord of death and also of rebirth. It just recently completed its transit in the sign in which it rules— Scorpio. During that transit we witnessed AIDS, ebola, much worldwide terrorism, child abductions, alien abductions, etc. Abduction is a Pluto theme, if you remember the rape of Persephone in Pluto's realm. Before awakenings take place, there is usually an upheaval in the subconscious. Pluto unearths hidden things and brings them into the light. Much psychotherapy deals with catharsis, a healing process whereby there is a release from fears hidden in the subconscious. The Latin *Pluton*, meaning the rich one, uncovers wealth hidden in the depths of the earth. This planet is now in the sign of Sagittarius which rules long distance travel, religion, philosophy and the legislative branch of the government. Most of our ways of thinking which we have all taken for granted will go through a Plutonian upheaval. Sagittarius is half-man and half-beast which implies a relationship between the body and the mind. Sports is one aspect of this duality. The O.J. Simpson case, as well as the Tanya Harding debacle, marked a recent signpost of Pluto's entry into Sagittarius. There will be further upheavals in the courts as well as in the church.

During the transit of Pluto through Scorpio it was closer to the sun than at any other time. Due to its elliptical orbit it has an aphelion and a perihelion. During the perihelion it entered the orbit of Neptune, thus fecundating that orbit. Pluto is the higher octave of Mars; both have a masculine polarity, Neptune is a feminine planet. Some astrologers believe that this portends an epochal change and a new birth.

Uranus is the harbinger of change and shatters the crystallised form of Saturn. When crystallised forms build up, electrical propensities begin to gather to shatter the form. This is uncomfortable to the human ego as well as outworn institutions. Uranus rules revolution and sudden changes which forward the evolution of the human spirit. For instance, the fall of the Berlin Wall (symbolised by Saturnian structures and boundaries) was during the passage of Uranus and Neptune in Capricorn.

Freedom is a strong Uranian theme which will become strongly emphasised during the passage of this planet through Aquarius as of January 1996. The state militias have recently been very vocal about the threat of our freedoms by the federal government bringing in foreign troops under the auspices of the United Nations. Similarly, the Republic of Chezenya is rebelling against the hegemony of Russia. Are they terrorists or are they freedom fighters? The issue of sovereignty should reside with the courts and not the battlefield.

Sagittarius is the sign of legislature and the higher courts. With the recent entry of Pluto into Sagittarius as of December 1995, there will be great upheavals in the judicial system. There is positive law which resides in our Constitution and judicial branches of our government and non-positive law which bypasses the Constitution. Freedoms which are guaranteed by the Constitution can be usurped by non-positive laws such as executive orders. Governments can suspend *habeas corpus* and other rights during martial law. All the government has to do is declare a state of emergency and the executive orders under FEMA come into effect. In such a case state sovereignty becomes extremely diminished. Should wide-scale rebellion occur, many individuals could be detained and imprisoned under the McCarron Act. This is not a prediction, but rather what some people fear.

Sagittarius, Capricorn, Aquarius and Pisces are universal signs, and the planets beyond Saturn are making their transits through these signs in the next few decades. Wide-scale change is inevitable and man will have to transcend his provincial ego to survive the changes. In the sign of Sagittarius, new ways of thinking will replace outworn paradigms, and new institutions represented by Capricorn will replace old ones. More equitable distribution of wealth will have to bridge the gap between the haves and have-nots in the sign of Aquarius. Lastly, man will have to overcome his inhumanity to his fellow man and learn humility and service under the sign of Pisces.

The time has come for change and reawakening of mankind and the human spirit. The present avatar Sathya Sai Baba will continue his mission to uplift humanity reestablishing the *dharma* (righteousness). During his next incarnation as Prema Sai, a new golden age will come into bloom around A.D. 2030. The world will be a better place with much of the present violence and competitiveness removed. Man will begin to see himself apart from his self-centred ego and recognise divinity as the motivating force in the world and himself.

One might question the validity of astrology since the stars and planets are far away. The whole universe is composed of light as God is light. Every variation of light creates a rhythm and all units of life and light are interconnected. Any change in rhythm where you are, effects changes in rhythm far, far away. The vast ocean of light is God and you are a wave in that ocean.

WHO IS SAI BABA?

Perhaps the greatest mystery of all is the divine incarnation. Eastern concepts of God are not too familiar in the West. The *Bhagavad Gita* states that when darkness threatens to overtake the world, God Himself takes the human form in order to save the *dharma* (righteousness). Lord Krishna was such an avatar in ancient India. Once again, in this age of *Kali* (darkness), the avatar has come, just as in the days of Krishna not everyone recognised him. Today, he resides in South India where anyone can travel to see him and obtain his *darshan*. He is recognised by millions of followers around the world of different faiths and backgrounds. He did not come to start a new religion or cult but to reestablish the ancient highway to God as laid down in the *Sanatana Dharma*.

There are many books written about the present Sathya Sai Baba and his previous incarnation as Shirdi Sai Baba. These books are published worldwide and anyone can obtain them. This chapter will only concern his avataric mission as prophesied by saints of modern and ancient times, in keeping with the title of this book—*Mysteries: Ancient and Modern*.

In the ancient Arabic book *Mehdi Moud* (Vol. 3 of the book: *Ocean of Light:* 14th Ed.) in which the prognostication made by the Prophet Mohammed had been recorded many centuries before, it was foreseen that God Himself would descend on Earth carrying the following signs of recognition:

HIS CLOTHING WILL BE LIKE A FLAME.

He will wear two robes.

His front teeth will be spaced apart.

His legs will be like those of a young girl.

His forehead will be large and concave.

His hair will be profuse.

His nose will be small with a slight hump at the bridge.

He will have a mole on his cheek.

The colour of his face will sometimes be like copper, sometimes yellow like gold, and sometimes shining like the moon.

He will give gifts that are light in weight.

His devotees will collect under a great tree.

He will go round amongst devotees and touch their heads with his hand.

All the treasures of the world will be under his feet.

All the things you will ask from God, he (the Master of the World) will give you.

All the teachings in the world will be in his heart from birth.

His devotees will crane their necks to see him.

He will live on a hill.

His house will be a square.

He will make the world light and full of grace.

Every eye that will see him will be happy, not only humans but disembodied souls.

He will live 95 years on Earth (Sai Baba says that he will retain his body until the 96th year; Indians, very logically call the actual day of birth the first birth date.

So as not to be deceived, you should know that the Master of the World will bring things out of his body through his mouth. (He manifests lingams from his body through his mouth.)

The above-mentioned signs of the avatar or God come to Earth as the Prophet Mohammed records in *Mehdi Moud* are directly applicable to Sri Sathya Sai Baba in every way, especially his physical description.

In the *Vishnu Puranas*, written over 5,000 years ago, it was prophesied that an avatar would incarnate in South India with all the powers of the godhead: that is, creation, preservation and destruction. He would be small in stature like Lord Krishna and his skin will be brown.

Over 400 years ago, Nostradamus wrote that a very great leader would be born in South India—land surrounded by three seas. He would have unlimited wisdom and power and would be the greatest conqueror in history. With his efforts, world war will be over and India's spiritual message to humanity would spread far and wide. He would be an immortal ruler. He would observe Thursday as the Holy Day.

In the *Shula Naadi*, a 5000-year-old palm leaf manuscript written by Sage Shula, today is a book written by Shantala Balu, entitled *Living Divinity* (1983, pp. 51-57). It describes Sage Shula's prophesies about Sai Baba.

He will be born for protecting and propagating dharma (righteousness) and he will have a mission to fulfil.

According to Shula, it was Kabir Das who returned to earth as Shirdi Sai Baba, who in turn came as Sathya Sai Baba, who will also return to earth as Prema Sai Baba.

He will be a great incarnation of Vishnu, having all powers of God.

Sri Sathya Sai Baba will perform great miracles.

One example mentioned in the Shula Naadi *is that he will keep an airplane airborne for a long time after it runs out of fuel through his will alone.*

He will always retain a youthful appearance, age notwithstanding.

> *He will be* Brahmachari *(celibate).*
> *He will have an equal attitude toward men and women. His glory will spread and many people will get near Him. But all will not receive grace due to past sins.*
> *He will establish educational institutions and hospitals (Sai Baba has opened many colleges and universities in India for men and women, and his hospitals are free of charge for bypass surgery and any other major illness).*

On Christmas Day in 1975, he revealed an astounding revelation before a group of Christians. In the following quote he overwhelmed the Christian world:

> *...There is one point that I cannot but bring to your special attention today. At the time when Jesus was merging in the supreme principle of divinity, he communicated some news to his followers which has been interpreted in a variety of ways by commentators and those who relish the piling of writings upon writings and meaning upon meaning, until it all swells up into a huge mess. The statement itself has been manipulated and tangled in a conundrum. The statement is simple:*
>
> *'He who sent me among you will come again...' and he pointed to a lamb. The lamb is merely a symbol, a sign. It stands for the voice 'ba-ba'. His name will be Truth. He wears a robe of red, a blood-red robe. (Here Baba pointed to the robe he was wearing). He will be short with a crown (of hair).'*

The lamb is the sign and symbol of love. Jesus said, "He who sent me will come again." That ba-ba is this Baba. Baba's first name is Sathya which means truth.

Sai Baba invites all to come and examine him. He says, "My life is my message." Man minus the ego is God, he declares. The goal of every soul is God-realisation. *Atma Vidya* (knowledge of one's *atma* or spirit) is *Brahma Vidya* (knowledge of God). God is the dweller in every heart, so there is no place to look except inside. Whether you understand the concept of an avatar does not matter, for God is all names and forms which the avatar embodies.

The avatar comes in human form so that mankind can aspire to divinity. No other avatar has done what this present avatar has demonstrated; that is, making himself available to all of mankind. He holds *darshan* twice a day and anyone can come to his *ashram*. He walks among us, consoling, uplifting, healing and performing miracles on a daily basis. The avatar has the ability to inaugurate a new era. He assures us that there will be a new golden age marked by peace and spirituality. Before his next incarnation, there will be a removal of those elements of chaos in society and a golden age will dawn.

In the meantime he advises us to see God in everyone. No one is high or low and the same God is the dweller in every heart. Love all and serve all. This he has consistently done and has trained his disciples to do. Service to man is the only way to serve God. Imagine when this becomes a worldwide reality.

Scatter the seeds of Love in dreary desert heart; then sprouts of Love will make the wastes green with joy, blossoms of Love will make the air fragrant, rivers of Love will murmur along the valleys, and every bird will beat, every child will sing the song of Love...

The service of man by man can lead to the discovery by man of the God that is his own reality.

SRI SATHYA SAI BABA

TALKING TO GOD

If it were not possible to talk directly to God then saints, sages, rishis and masters of all times would not have been able to do so. The truth is that anyone can talk directly to God; however, one cannot do so through the sensory mind. It is through the soul-mind within the silence that anyone can talk to God.

> The more and more each is impelled by that which is intuitive, the relying upon the soul-force within, the greater, the farther, the deeper, the broader, the more constructive may be the result.
>
> **EDGAR CAYCE 792-2**

Cayce explained that the "mind is the builder", so the key lies in the focus on the mind. Now, the mind can go in two directions, outward toward the senses, or inward toward the soul. When we think of our minds we usually think only of our conscious self and believe that it is only this part of our mind which makes all of our decisions. This is simply not so. The conscious mind is only that aspect of ourselves which we are aware of, yet there is more to the mind which affects us than our conscious self.

Whatever is the dominant desire in the subconscious mind, it is that desire which will rule and dominate the conscious mind. The conscious mind cannot put any idea or desire into action until it has the permission of the subconscious mind. How many of us are aware of the contents of our subconscious mind? This is the real person. Habits deeply ingrained in the subconscious mind continue to dominate our lives no matter how much "will-power" our conscious mind exerts in our affairs. The subconscious mind works like a computer programme and much that is in there was placed there even before we became conscious of it. The subconscious mind believes what was placed there by the conscious mind at the time it believed it and will not be changed even though the conscious mind no longer believes it unless the programme is changed in the subconscious. This change in the subconscious can only occur when the conscious mind is bypassed. By setting aside our conscious mind, that is, temporarily shut down our sensory body-mind, we can then effect a change in our conscious mind.

For instance, if your belief is that only holy people can talk directly to God, then that will be part of your embedded subconscious programme. A new idea, that you are a child of God and are wholly worthy to talk to him, must be continually reinforced until it becomes entrenched as a habit in your thinking. Obviously, then, you must temporarily set aside your conscious critical mind, so that thinking from this false premise can be stopped; thus, a correct assumption can be replaced for the false one stored in the subconscious.

The subconscious mind makes a good servant and a poor master. Whatsoever your subconscious mind believes makes the difference between success or failure, happiness or misery, health or illness. Think of the subconscious mind as your foundation. In this foundation resides your deepest desires and emotions. This is the driving force in your life, not what you are consciously thinking of at the moment. We are solely at the mercy of our subconscious minds and answer to its behest unless we learn to master it. If you have a goal in mind, you will not be able to move toward that goal unless you remove the subconscious impediments. The subconscious mind is not trained to think but to carry out its programme. In order to talk to God, you must not talk in words but through your deepest desire. This desire must be placed in your subconscious.

So, the first step is desire in the subconscious. There is no thinking involved. You must concentrate your thinking mind to the stillness of the zero point. The zero point is that place of stillness, no thinking. "Be still and know I am God." Meditation is another word for no-mind. Do not think about God, feel Him and allow yourself to know Him. If you think about Him then you divide yourself from Him as in subject and object. God is light and so are you. Allow yourself to feel the Oneness. Now, this is no longer a reality of your thinking-mind but your soul-mind. You are no longer thinking about worldly things but are now in spirit.

Now you are in the heavens and are no longer in the world. You no longer sense through your mind but rather through your soul and become more wholly (mind-soul) mind. You are less of your body and are more your soul. You are bathed in light and beauty and are in harmony with the rhythm of the universe. You are a "dreamer" and not a sensor.

You suddenly realise that you are in communion with God, and feel the Oneness, the love. You are also One with all that is, and feel the pulse of the universe. You know that God is love and so are you. You know your God-self and the finite you (mortal) has become the infinite and eternal You. Whatever you desired to know, you know now and whatever you wanted you have. When you are at oneness with all things, you have all things. You and your Father are One. God does not give you all things, but merely allows you to become aware that you always possessed the knowledge and power in the first place.

The Creator gives you the tools, but you must learn to use them and share, by equal giving, with the universe. The universal laws are based upon rhythmic balanced interchange. God will always work with you, but you must work for Him first. By putting Him first you remain in harmony with the universe.

You have now arrived. You have stepped out of the body
of yourself into the soul-mind of yourself. You are no longer
just the material body with its sensory needs and demands but
are and forever remain the soul. You have not stepped out of
reality but into true reality. You have journeyed out of the
divided, conditioned universe, into the undivided,
unobstructed universe. You are now mind-knowing and not
mind-sensory thinking. God has given you illumination from
the realm of divine ideas and you are inspired. You can take
the conceptual idea of this thought into manifestation. Once
you know the cause behind this world of effects, you can take
this mind-knowing into your life as reality.

Your body is the result of your mind-thinking. If you are
ill, then you can change the effects by changing the cause.
You are eternal balance, the real you. You can change
imbalance in the body, your mortal self, by centring in your
immortal Self. No one can do this for you.

One must remember God's laws even in prayer and
meditation. The universe is based on the law of balance. One
cannot ask God for peace, happiness, money or anything
without that balance being replaced on earth. If you ask for
peace, you must live peacefully. If you ask for money, you
must not be selfish with its use.

Talking to God must come from the heart or it is not
answered. If the prayer on the lips is just repeated with no
heartfelt feeling, then it assuredly will not be heard. Prayer or
meditation cannot be accomplished through the sensory
mind, it must come from the soul. Prayer is talking to God or
making the invocation. Meditation is listening to God for the
evocation or response. Neither can be accomplished without
the desire and quieting the senses.

The word trance has been given a negative meaning.
When you transcend your body-mind you are in a sort of
trance. Note the word transcend in the previous sentence.
Yes, you must transcend your earthly awareness to achieve a
spiritual awareness. Trance is also used in hypnosis. To

change the faulty programming in the subconscious, you must bypass or transcend the conscious mind. There is nothing mystifying about this process, nor is there any reason to fear.

LIFE IS THE
BATTLEFIELD

If one is illiterate, never reads a book, nor ever finds a teacher or guru, he or she can still learn in the school of life. Life is the greatest teacher and initiator. The learned and the scholarly in every field still suffer from a horrible disease, namely, the underdevelopment of the moral imperative. What good is knowledge if it leads into the morass of moral degeneracy? Our vaunted knowledge has not solved the mysteries of life, death and liberation.

Life is a battlefield according to the *Bhagavad Gita*. Duties and desires are perpetually in conflict. The wants and the cravings of the ego are endless and often interfere with one's *dharma*. The goal of liberation can only be obtained when we rid ourselves of all the excess baggage of attachment which we carry with us from life to life. A question was posed to the sleeping Edgar Cayce as to what happens to a soul if it fails to improve itself in life. The reading stated:

> *That's why the reincarnation, why it reincarnates;*
> *that it may have the opportunity. Can the will of*
> *man continue to defy its maker?*
> **EDGAR CAYCE 826-8**

Coming down into the field of *karma*, duality is inevitable and conflict ensues. Man has to pay his debts. The world into which he is born has to be watched and studied with diligence; the word "world" means everything that is not the Self. Life is the field *(kshetra)* where the battle is fought. The Self is the knower and wages battle with the not-self. That one has to be in the world and not of the world is what all of the world's scriptures attest. Activity which is devoid of reverence and humility leads to authoritarianism, audacity and arrogance; hence, the reason for all of the cruelty in the world. True soul-culture is permeated with an atmosphere of humility, awe, and holiness.

Mutual respect can only be built on the faith that all are children of the Divine, irrespective of religion, caste or race. On the basis of harmony and cooperation, can each soul fulfil his dharma in the world? The rapacious greed and lack of cooperation today, as evidenced in a materialistic culture, harms the weak, rapes the environment and stifles the spirit.

A devotee of Sai Baba once asked him that if life is all *Sat-Chit-Ananda* or existence, consciousness and bliss, then why is there so much pain and misery in the world? Sai Baba answered by saying that if one does not know the darkness, then how could one understand the light? It is not enough to know that fire burns, there must be the experience of pain to bring that recognition to reality. *Karma* has to be done, there can be no turning away from the fruits of one's actions.

Life is always the teacher. The toddler learns to walk on its own by first stumbling and much of life is learned by trial and error; however, once something is mastered there is no need to repeat the same mistakes. Each has been assigned a task according to merit from previous lives, status, taste, character, etc. We are all actors on the stage of life. God assigns each soul a part to play in the drama of life and He knows the outcome from the beginning.

There is the story of the country bumpkin who goes to the city to watch a play. The play might contain a scene which closely parallels his own life. He gets so caught up in the drama which is unfolding before his eyes that he leaps forward to participate in the drama, unaware that it is just the unfolding of a script written to be acted out on stage. The characters are just acting the scene allotted to them, backed by a choreographer and musicians.

Every day that we wake up, we must feel that we are entering the stage of life to play the role which God has assigned to us. The ego is the actor and not the author of the script. If the ego believes itself to be the "doer", then it is no different from the country bumpkin. The field of life is the field of activity and one must recognise the God within as the prompter and the *raison d'etre* of that activity. We have to travel along the path of *karma* to *dharma* to reach *Brahman*.

It is the attachment to the fruits of action that binds a soul in time. Equal detachment should be given to success or failure if *dharma* or right action is followed. Surrender of the ego as the doer is the only way to liberation. Caught in time the soul is given a life sentence and a long journey to the grave. Like any prisoner, we are circumscribed by cause and effect, age, deteriorisation of the body and decay. The problem resides with identification of the body as the sole reality. We have to use the body as a ferryman uses a boat to cross a river. Death has been compared to the river Styx and in Indian philosophy, an ocean of *samsara*.

> *What makes you think that 'doing' is so important? Be equal-minded. Then you will not be bothered about 'doing' or 'not-doing', success or failure; the balance will remain unaffected by either. Let the wave of memory, the storm of desire, the fire of emotion pass through without affecting your equanimity. Be a witness of these. Commitment engenders holding, narrowing, limiting. Be willing to be nothing. Let all dualities subside in your neutrality.*
>
> SATHYA SAI BABA

Does life have to be a battlefield? Richard Nixon once said that there are no antecedents in history for peace, so the inevitability of war has to be prepared for. It all depends on how the battle is waged. Mahatma Gandhi used the principle of *Sathya Graha* or the "force of truth". Since warfare is often fought with deception, then the force of truth has to be employed. The battle is really with the lower self. Desire has to be transmuted into aspiration, passion into compassion, and pain and suffering into joy.

The problem really lies with faulty vision. Duality and conflict disappear when the correct vision of Oneness is held. This is the teaching of *Advaita Vedanta* or non-dualism. Since there is only the One playing all the roles, our correct vision is to hold on to the One and play the role assigned to us with detachment and surrender. Opposites or extremes meet or merge into each other in the ocean of love.

For there to be peace and equal-mindedness, then there must be some kind of mind control. Since the rapid growth of knowledge which is increasing in the Aquarian Age, the mind is highly engaged and becomes restless. The battlefield of life must be waged by control of the mind and the senses.

The interval between the mind's passing from one idea to another—the period of calm between the two storms of Thought—may be described as the condition of the Self.

YOGAVASISHTHA

Meditation may be described as the interval between two thoughts. Yoga is the control of the thinking principle. What one does and what one thinks, he truly becomes. The mind-stuff or *chitta* is easily agitated, especially when directed toward the world and the senses.

> *Fix thy mind on That which is not smitten with the evil eye of the Devil of Multifariousness, causing shakiness of mind.*
>
> YOGAVASISHTHA

Once the vision is corrected, then the battlefield of life becomes an adventure and not a tragedy. The impurities must first be corrected in the mind. The Edgar Cayce readings are replete with advice on how to accomplish this:

> *Know the first principles: There is good in all that is alive.*
>
> CAYCE 2537-1
>
> *From what may anyone be saved? Only from themselves! That is their individual hell; they dig it with their own desires.*
>
> CAYCE 5125-1
>
> *Rather, then, than the stars ruling life, the life should rule the stars. For man was created a little bit higher than all the rest of the whole universe, and is capable of harnessing, directing, enforcing the laws of the universe.*
>
> CAYCE 5-2

THE MYSTERY OF
WAVES

The glyph for Aquarius is two parallel wavy lines. Lines have a forward vector and wavy lines have a forward and a lateral vector. The forward vector implies progression. God's first law is forward progression. All souls are on the path of progression. What appears to be retrogression, or backward motion, is an illusion. We are waves riding on the ocean of bliss and what appears to be our subsidence is also an illusion since we remain in the ocean to arise again.

Then, there is the ocean of electromagnetism which is merely a compilation of various waves. The universe was created with light and sound which are merely waves. In the stillness there is no movement. In the creation, there is nothing but movement. Life is a series of appearances of waves, and death is the cessation of appearances. The mystery of waves is locked up in the mystery of life and death. Nothing is destroyed but merely transformed. Between the physical level of existence and the energy level of existence there is an interconnectedness. Matter and energy are interchangeable and so are life and death. Just as in the symbol of yin and yang the wave contains the whole Tao.

This wave is illustrated in the systolic and diastolic beat of the heart, in the inhalation and the exhalation of breath and the rising and setting of the sun. Since we live in the plane of duality, the wave represents this idea. The primary idea inherent in the wave is movement or progression. The universe consists of only waves in motion. The system which creates these waves is centripetal and centrifugal. Time can be compared to a wave motion of events. Just as a series of pictures in a cinema is speeded up to represent action on a screen, so time is a wave motion of events. Time is merely a record of changing events in pulse motion of a wave. Einstein postulated that once you travel the speed of light which is a wave motion, then time itself starts to flow backward. The senses only record time in its forward motion; however, if, as Einstein said, time can flow backward as well, we do not perceive this to be true. Just as in every wave motion, the forward progression and the backward recession cancel each other out.

Life and death are just as illusory as the cinemas we witness on our entertainment screens. The *Bhagavad Gita* states that no one is ever born and no one ever dies. Time and space really do not exist except to the senses. The soul stands outside of time in the *Eternal Now*. Perhaps, this is the reason why man accepts *maya* (unreality) for reality. This is also the reason why sense-based science cannot fathom the truth behind the universe.

As a separate entity we function as the wave in the ocean of life. Just as waves rise and fall in the ocean, so too do we rise and fall. As a wave, we are always changing and can do nothing to change this fact. We want permanency but can do nothing except flow with this change. It is the nature of a wave to be in motion as there is nothing static in the universe. Only the ocean is permanent not the wave. A Buddha is not in the future or in the past: he has ceased to be the wave and has become the ocean. Our sense organs are just doors and windows of perception. We do not see with our eyes, hear with our ears or touch with our hands.

> *The fifteen rays return into their source: the divine forces governing the senses find back the universal fountain of their rise; the reflection in the inner sense—the embodied soul—together with every action whatever, all become one in the supreme unchangeable Essence. As rivers flow into the ocean and lose their individual name and form, nay thus lose even themselves, so does the knower, freed from all name and form, find the highest Being, all light.*
> *He who thus knows the highest Self, verily becomes Self; none that is born in family has his eyes closed to Self. He soars above sin and sorrow; freed from the ties of the heart, he becomes immortal.*
>
> **MUNDAKA UPANISHAD**

Whenever you sense through your eyes, remember the inner you. Whenever you sense through the ears, remember who is the one that hears. If you think through the brain, ascertain who is doing the thinking. We are not our organs of perception, these are merely our tools. A seer looks above, beyond and past the senses all the way to *Brahman*, the essence of all things. A true seer sees all waves as the ocean.

Only the formless is eternal. All forms have a birth and a death in the cycles of nature. If you fell yourself as a body, a form, you get into difficulty. If you feel yourself as the ocean and not the wave, then you can begin to feel the unending, undiminished bliss. We fear death, but death is the other side of life. If you hold onto the wave and feel yourself separate from the ocean fear arises. The "I am the body (wave) idea" has to be replaced with "I am the ocean" idea.

> *These rivers flowing to and gaining the ocean lose themselves in it, lose even their name and form, and become included in the name 'Ocean.'*

> *So do all the sixteen forms of the objective flowing to and gaining the Self become lost in Him. They lose even their name and form, and become included in the Self. This Self is the immortal, transcending all forms of the mortal. This is thus summed up: That death not overpower thee, know the only unknowable, the Self, in whom are centred all forms like the radii of a chariot wheel in its hub.*
>
> PRASHNO UPANISHAD

Aquarius is the sign of the Water Bearer but is not a water sign. The two way lines represent the etheric waters. Aquarius is a universal sign and its reflexive sign, Leo, is the sign of the individual. Solar radiation unites with cosmic radiation and all become one. As long as there is creation there will be waves. There are basically three types of energy in the universe: dynamic, electromagnetic and frictional electricity. The dynamic electricity, called *Fohat* by the Egyptians, is the cosmic energy which makes galaxies spin. This is forward motion. Electromagnetic energy is spiralic and is the energy that makes planets orbit the sun. Frictional electricity is the lowest form and represents our fossil fuels. This motion is circular. They equal spirit, soul and matter, respectively. As we move more into the Aquarian Age, the electromagnetic energy of waves will be tapped.

The soul is electromagnetic, and the double helix spiral of *kundalini* which runs up man's spine is depicted by a Caduceus. Another way to describe this energy is a standing column wave like Nicola Tesla's Tesla Coil. Pyramids produce similar energy and perhaps this was the secret of Atlantean science.

In the Huna religion, the power of *manna* is represented by wavy lines. Huna magic, like other forms of magic, utilises the etheric plane. According to Huna, the substance of this plane is called "aka". This aka is sticky and adheres to all material objects forming a giant matrix covering the earth which the Huna call the "Great Po Aumakua". Tachyons which have been recently discovered as faster than light particles also stick or tack on to objects. Perhaps, this is the basis for psychometry, where a psychic picks up an object and "reads" the object based on the energy deposits adhering to it.

Life is measured in pulsations or waves as attested by our medical equipment. Variations in waves can determine whether we are telling the truth according to polygraph tests. Seismographs record shock waves from earthquakes. Waves measure energy, life, motion and impacts from shock.

A whole new age will emerge when the new Aquarian science masters the use of waves as it has done already in laser technology. There is more yet to come.

THE MYSTERY OF
SPIRALS

Spirals in nature show up repeatedly, from the double-helix in DNA to Spiral Nebula. It would appear that there are no boxes in the universe, only curves. The major premise of the previous chapter was that waves represent motion or progression. In the creation, nothing is static and everything is in motion; however, this motion is not in a straight line. Light bends, space is curved, so motion in a straight line is bent into curves and spirals.

All orbits, whether subatomic or macrocosmic, are curved and rotate. This same principle which characterises the universe can be seen in embryology as the embryo grows in a spiral around the navel. The four-armed *swastika*, which is really an ancient Hindu symbol, symbolises the spiralic nature of this rotation. Every rotation does so on an axis or central point. From the central point the spiral goes in two directions centripetally and centrifugally, according to the law of polarity.

When the Absolute divided itself from itself, it became both subject and object. The axis between these two poles formed the *Axis Mundi* or the pole of the world. Our axis is our spine which is our link to heaven and earth. The *kundalini*, coiled serpent, is a spiral. The expansion and contraction are the spiralling inward and spiralling outward forces of the universe. From the central *bindu*, or point of axis, everything is hyper-extended, radiates and rotates spirally. The whole entire universe is a giant rotation spirally from a centre of stillness. From this still point, rotation expands outward and then spirals inward to disappear from whence it came. You might say it is a simultaneous movement in both directions at once. Another way of describing how the unmanifest becomes manifest is that from the unmanifest, motion flows in a circle and returns from whence it came.

As a thinker and creator yourself, you envision an idea reasoning from the general to the particular on the outgoing spiral (centrifugal) and then reason from the particular to the general on the inward spiral (centripetal). So there is first a focus of power at a point (*bindu*) and this is called concentration. Secondly, there is an extension of this power spirally, so that consciousness is extended outwardly. Manifestation implies definition, limitation and circumscription. Circles are spirals when manifesting outwardly. The universe is a manifestation of wheels within wheels, the one circumscribed by its creations, within other ones circumscribed by its creations. *Karma* is a circle. The outgoing spirallic thought returns to the sender on its inward return.

Man's destiny in the scheme of things is to connect heaven and earth. The descending spiral of spirit into matter is the *bindu* on the top of the head. Man is that contraction or limitation of spirit into matter. On the ascending arc, the spiral upward is the path of return of outward expansion or spiralling upward from the coils of manifestation. The point of intersection of these two spirals of whirling vortices is best represented by the Seal of Solomon. This is man's state in balance and equilibrium.

Now to fully understand this double spin, we have to look at the *vajra*, or "diamond sceptre" in Tibetan Buddhism. This *vajra* shows the union of opposites. The original point or *bindu*, while remaining fixed and centred, spirals outward toward the periphery. This is union with the subjective and the objective. The subjective is the fixed *bindu* point and the objective is the balancing of the pairs of opposites on the outward path.

To understand how order comes from disorder one has to look at the creation of the diamond. Diamonds consist of the same atoms of graphite, yet, in the diamond state the diamond is colourless and contains all colours, it can cut anything while nothing can cut it. Jewels have clarifying power and can bring coherency out of incoherence.

The spiral shapes of cones also signify coherency. The coned unicorn is one of the symbols of the third eye, when opened. The ancient ziggurats represented the spiralling nature of consciousness. From the base of matter or the base of a cone, matter accumulates and multiplies this accumulation as it spirals up the cone's apices. Radioactivity is the ascent of this spiral and electricity is the descent of the collapsing spiral. Both the ascending and descending arc from the life-death cycle of the universe.

Nature is curved, space is curved, and spheres are radial spirals of balanced centripetal and centrifugal forces. All spheres rotate when thrown in space. If you throw a rock or a snowball, it will start spinning as soon as it leaves your arm. Most explosions are radiative; that is, they extend outward from a centre. Such explosions in reverse are called implosions and have far greater power. Both creation and destruction can be viewed spirally. The combination of these two forces in equilibrium are what holds matter together. The variations of these spins of wave amplitudes are the forces which generate or degenerate matter. The senses do not record matter as waves and spirals. Nevertheless, all of life consists of waves upon waves of various amplitudes; circles with circles and spirals within spirals.

If you seriously think about it, your life is a series of spirals and orbits. From the centre of your home, you radially and spirally extend yourself and your life outward and then withdraw inward toward the centre at the close of the day. Your time may be viewed as events extending spirally away from and toward your home. Sufi dancing also represents the winding and the unwinding of the universe. In fact, the whole journey from the microcosm to the macrocosm may be seen as an axis along a giant spiral.

The ascending and descending spiral of Jacob's ladder shows the ascent of man's soul and the descent of the divine light. Spirals lead us from visibility to invisibility. Was this knowledge known in antiquity? Perhaps this knowledge was revealed in the Chinese text, *The Secret of the Golden Flower,* which describes the spirallic circulation of the light in the third eye. Or, perhaps, the knowledge of spirallic force was known in Glastonbury as the Dragon Current where the energy of the earth spirals in certain places. Also, many *mandalas* in Tibet, Bhutan, and Southeast Asia depict spirallic forces.

The centripetal and centrifugal forces can easily be seen in the way water spins down the drain in your bathtub. It does so clockwise in the Northern Hemisphere and counterclockwise in the Southern Hemisphere. The trajectory of rockets will lean in the same direction when shot from the equator toward the Northern or Southern hemispheres. This is why geosynchronous orbits can only be achieved when fired from or nearest to the equator.

Our descent into this world and our return to spirit is perhaps the greatest spiral of all. At death, the long, dark tunnel is seen as a spiral.

> *As a hawk or an eagle, having soared high in the air, wings its way back to its resting place, being so far fatigued, so does the soul, having experienced the phenomenal, return into Itself where it can sleep beyond all desires, beyond all dreams.*
>
> **BRIHADARANYAKA UPANISHAD**

PROPHECY

Prophecy is usually proven unacceptable until the prophet has been correct. The ancient Hebrews used to stone their prophets if any of their predictions were proven incorrect. To objectify what has not occurred but what is about to occur has always been inscrutable and continues to be, hence, remains a perennial mystery to be solved along with other ageless mysteries.

The problem resides in what we consider the objective world in the first place, which is merely the world of the senses and of appearances. Hasn't Eastern philosophy told us not to trust our senses and that the world of maya is not to be believed? How then does the seer truly see beyond the confines of time and space?

The previous two chapters describe the wave and spiralic nature of the universe. Time itself is like a giant corkscrew. What is a prophet except one who can apprehend the shadow which the future casts in the present. The prophet is living proof of the fact that time is a complete unity. Remember the wave is a progression and the spiral is both progression and circular. In this cyclic view of time, the present moment is both a point and also part of a cycle which is in relationship with other cycles; all wheels within wheels. The present is the pivotal point in which is balanced the past and the future.

Imagine a rocket travelling toward infinity in a straight line. At the apex of this rocket is a long rod. According to general relativity, the front part of this rod at the end of the rocket would accelerate faster than the part joined to the rocket. Also, according to this theory, the space-time illustration which describes this accelerating rocket would be curved with respect to the rest of the universe; that is, it would take the form of two cones (spirals) apex to apex. Where these centripetal and centrifugal forces meet forms the simultaneous nature of all the events which took place in that rocket ship.

The ancient Hindus were correct when they believed that the entire being of all created things was balanced upon a single point (*bindu*). Past, present and future are all one where these two cones meet. Most clairvoyants are able to see beyond time and space because they are able to tap into that spot (point, *bindu*, third eye, blue pearl, etc.) between their eyes. By focussing on their own soul, third eye, the prophet is able to link up with the destiny of other souls.

Pyramids are also time chambers. The all-seeing eye at the apex of the pyramid as seen on the dollar bill represents this idea. The mysteries of the pyramids have yet to be unveiled. Not only do they contain time capsules, but their very shape may be the key to cross over the barriers of time and space.

Both the ascending and descending spirals meet at the apex of the pyramid. The inward thrust of gravity meets the outward thrust of radiation at the pyramid's apex. Both clockwise spirals and anti-clockwise spirals are the reverse of each other, yet each comes from the other without a reversal in direction. What appears to be the illusion of time is the sequence of life-death cycles.

Since every point in space is connected to every other point in space, what happens anywhere appears to happen everywhere. The prophet merely turns into the great cosmic cinema of space-time. This universe is *maya* or a universe of what seems to be, a world of appearances. The void or that which is described in Buddhism is really the zero universe of reality. The zero point or omega point is that reality of oneness which transcends or voids all duality in the plus or minus range. Just as a mirage of images of light and darkness is focused on the cinema screen, so too is the entire space-time script projected from the zero point. There is a simultaneous movement in both directions away from the zero point and back again.

Upon death, the whole circumference of the events of one's life is revealed simultaneously as in a panorama; you are the *bindu* or point of consciousness at the centre. The 'Christ-consciousness is always the present moment which contains both the past and the future. Prophets are essentially lords of time. Prophecy means to speak from divine inspiration and some prophets are unable to even interpret what they say. Edgar Cayce, for instance, did not understand the meaning or the content of his prophesies when in his waking state.

Some prophesies can be calculated, such as the procession of the equinoxes which determine the astrological year. The equinoctial points move one degree every 72 years which, when multiplied by the circumference degrees in a circle (360), gives you the Great Year or *Annus Magnus*— approximately 26,000 years. We are presently at the end of an *Annus Magnus* or 26,000-year cycle with the culmination of the Piscean Age. The *Yugas* are also a way of calculating time and prophesying what will occur. This present *Kali Yuga* is called the Iron Age and is marked by misery, dishonesty and death. Only 25 per cent of the human population are *dharmic* (righteous) during the *Kali* period. These *Yugas* last for vast periods of time, approximately 360,000 years. Fortunately, according to Sri Yukteswar who was the guru to Paramahamsa Yogananda, we are leaving the *Kali Yuga* and entering the *Dwapara Yuga* (Copper Age). God reveals Himself during each succeeding *Yuga* from gross energy to subtle energy.

Every cycle is a spirallic progression. The last Aquarian Age was during Atlantis which was marked by scientific achievement and great knowledge. This present Aquarian

Age is another turn of the spiral and will carry with it some of the same *karmic* lessons. According to Edgar Cayce, most of the souls from Atlantis are presently reincarnated.

Some prophecy is not calculated by time but is channeled. In ancient times, these prophets were called Sybils, oracles or diviners. Just as a medical prognosis is a prediction of sorts, so too does a seer make a prognosis based upon his visions or precognitive awareness. Some of today's channelers claim to be in contact with ascended masters, E.T.s or other cosmic entities. Another theory is that a psychic or channeler may just be tuning into what Carl Jung calls the collective unconscious.

Now, clairvoyance or "clear-seeing" is an extended sense of sight. The old teachings of Tibet claim that there are five different kinds of eyes beside the human. The first is that of beast or birds who possess eyes of instinct. Sometimes the eyes of animals are even greater than humans'. The second is celestial eyes whose sight is capable of seeing humans and their own domain at the same time. These are the *devas* or celestial gods and goddesses. They can also see the past and future births of beings over many lifetimes. The third category is those who possess eyes of Truth like the *Bodhisattvas*. A *Bodhisattva* is a perfected being who is liberated but chooses to stay with humanity to guide the race. These beings can see backward and forward in time over many world periods: *kalpas, manvantaras, yugas*, etc. The fourth type of eyesight is the Divine which the more advanced adepts possess. They can see through millions of world periods. Lastly, the fifth type of-vision is possessed by the eyes of wisdom of Buddhas who can see throughout eternity.

> *Nothing would be uncertain and the future, as the past, would be present to [our] eyes.*
>
> PIERRE DE LAPLACE

THE MYSTERY OF
ZERO

> *NOTHING CAN BE CREATED OUT OF NOTHING.*
>
> LUCRETIUS

As stated in earlier chapters, centrifugal force comes in to counterbalance the centripetal force of gravity. The nature of zero comes in when one cancels the other out. Radiation is a one-way ticket to death and the counterbalancing inward force cancels out the complete entropy of the universe. It is like God looking in the mirror and never seeing the other half of Himself.

The centrifugal force is not different or separate from the centripetal force. They are interdependent and exist only in the process of their dialectical combination. Their divergence takes place from the zero point in a plus or minus direction. For instance, the same light waves bouncing off the mirror are the reverse of the original image due to an illusion that the image is replicated in the manner in which it is presented. The zero point is the place where seeming polarity divides.

Another fact of nature which Galileo so aptly demonstrated from the Leaning Tower of Pisa is that all objects dropped from the tower together hit the ground together. It did not make a difference whether the objects were light or heavy. The difference in their arrival time at the ground is accepted as exactly zero. This is known as the equivalence principle; that is, a principle of gravity which requires that the gravitational response of a body is independent of the nature of that body. Now if all matter was rapidly expanding away from each other as in the Big Bang Theory, eventually the universe would fizzle out; however, if a counterbalancing force were equal to that original force then the difference would be zero.

Just as we look into the mirror and do not perceive our image reversal, so too, under the illusion of time moving only forward, do we not perceive the backward motion voiding out time to the zero point. Time has no existence except in this apparent reversal of motion. We live in a zero universe and all else is only apparent effects. The still zero point of consciousness exists whether we are alive or dead. Consciousness persists after death and creates both time and space for its environments.

It is the stillness of gravity which centres motion. It is the wave-electric universe which is in motion. The omnipresent zero or stillness point of gravity centres the centrifugal and centripetal waves of motion. It is the electric rings which encircle gravity that have motion. It is electricity which is motion, and the magnetic light of stillness centres that motion. All is held in the mind of God as a seed idea. The seed, like zero, is nothing yet contains all things. In Hinduism, the concept of the creation of the universe lies in the Brahmin Egg, a zero with the whole included. Division by zero is impossible; it is like dividing by everything or dividing by nothing.

There is always a point of stillness which centres around every action. That point of stillness is the zero centring point. Motion spins in axial rotation around that still point, but there is not any motion at the centre. Between two poles of any sphere, at that centre point, there is zero potential. Likewise, every thought and action in the universe is centred by its still point of emergence. This still point of emergence controls thoughts and actions from within and balances them from without by two extensions of the centre.

Gravity and magnetism both belong to the zero universe. Electricity belongs to the wave universe. Gravity is the central point of stillness in the invisible universe. It is this point or *bindu* which is the seed from which the electric wave of the universe sprouts. It is this still point which is the centre of the mind universe which contains the germinal ideas of thought creation. Mind is that centre which balances, controls, peruses, or stimulates in action the idea which exists in the stillness by fast or slow motion. You cannot see gravity or mind, but you can locate it at the centre of every created thought ring. At the moment when electricity divides the one changeless condition into pairs, it is necessary to control these pairs. It is gravity or the point of magnetic stillness which is the controller and balance of these pairs. Wherever motion is, it is centred by stillness and that stillness is CAUSE. We are used to living in the world of effects.

Everything in the relative world is forever moving and changing. Whatever begins, ends. Like images in a mirror, all things, entities and processes within nature are ephemeral. If we are to pursue that which is changeless, constant and forever remaining the same in a changing, endless rearranging universe, then we are pursuing God or the Tao. Characteristics of the absolute are in contrast to the characteristics of the emerging creation. All things, all beings and all phenomena are only the modification of the pre-existing Tao. The ultimate stuff is at the centre or core of the relative world, while remaining outside and beyond the relative world. It precedes the world in a form opposite to the one it takes in the relative world, yet it is continuous with this realm. This oneness contains no two things or no distinctions and no duality, yet the ten thousand things or many things are characterised by all of these.

This zero or no-thing is a state of rest with infinite velocity; it is the ultimate, infinite which contains great frequency, amplitude and force. Since it is infinite, it does not conform to our finite senses. The duality of time and space do not exist in this realm. Like all things of infinite speed and velocity, it is invisible to the mortal eye. To know it is to know it with the intuitive faculties of the mind. The two poles of yin and yang emerge from this point within the expanse of infinity. The currents and streams of energy and movement meet and interact at a geometric point. Hence, all antagonistic-complementary dualism of the phenomenal world are just the two faces—or the front and back—of one ultimate reality.

The spiral is a two-dimensional representation, whereas the helix is three-dimensional. Both arise from a central point (*bindu*) of manifestation. Extension or motion is a wave (electrical) from a central point (magnetic) of stillness. Electrical potential is zero at the centre where no wave exists and increases at the periphery. Knowing how the zero universe of cause works, man in the future will be able to master the world of effects. We travel in consciousness as the seed ideas of creation exist in the mind of the creator and man. In spirit, one merely has to think and it is done. If you think of a location, you are there; there is no time lapse in your doing. Indeed, the mystery of zero is a great mystery. Matter and anti-matter may truly be mirror images of each other constituting a whole. Man and the cosmos are but mirror image reflections of each other with the whole constituting the Tao. Man exists wherever form and spirit meet. The mind of man, like the mind of God, is the centring still magnetic point (zero) which balances the dialectic. When man understands the zero universe, he will be able to travel the vast reaches of space by collapsing time.

METANOIA

A new type of thinking is essential if mankind is to survive and move toward higher levels.

ALBERT EINSTEIN

How do we arrive at higher levels of consciousness in our present state of development? Aldous Huxley considered our consciousness part and parcel of a larger one. We live in a sea of energy, a sea of consciousness and a sea of mind. Our so-called normal consciousness is that which is funnelled through our sensory brain-mind as a bio-transducer. We are protected, so to speak, from a total inundation of the whole sea coming through a dyke. R.D. Laing, a Scottish psychiatrist, believes that this valve mechanism which controls consciousness may be lost in the schizophrenic. A schizophrenic may be having a breakthrough rather than a breakdown. The question remains, can consciousness be structured and allowed to grow and change or is sensory reality a permanent fixture? Organs of perception seem to evolve so as to perceive more of reality. It was not believed that early man on the planet had a highly developed colour sense. He may have been colour blind.

We develop a view of the world since childhood and build up our field of conceptual reality and oftentimes are unable to change these concepts. It is inherent in the nature of structure or conceptualised models of thinking to have built-in limitations. To awake from a former way of thinking one must have a conversion of some kind. The Greek word *metanoia* translates as a fundamental transformation of mind. Old concepts are replaced and a reshaping of the mind takes place. A conversion takes place when the mind is seized upon an idea that orients us around a single focal point of possibility, just as Archimedes exclaimed "I have found it," or "Eureka".

This centring of the mind fills a person with conviction and power which creates saints, genius, martyrs or Nazis. Power lies in concentrated thinking which precipitates into the material world. As anyone who has studied molecular physics knows, the pressure of a gas increases with a rise in temperature, while the volume remains constant. A rise in temperature is due to increase in molecular vibration. Just for this reason, the higher you raise the calibre of a thought within the confines of your brain, the greater is the pressure so produced. This is the reason for silence. Every thought you keep to yourself is in the process of precipitation. Every thought you carelessly release to others is dissipated.

However, it should also be considered that any power strong enough to create could equally destroy. We all know what concentrated negative thinking can produce. Nothing can harm you except the evil you harbour within yourself. Whatever has the seeds of destruction within itself will destroy itself. The world, thus far, knows how to create death, now we must learn how to live. This will take a *metanoia* or a new way of thinking.

> *Right mindfulness snatches the pearl of Freedom from the Dragon Time.*
>
> **HEART OF BUDDHIST MEDITATION**
>
> *I didn't arrive at my understanding of the fundamental laws of the universe through my rational mind.*
>
> **ALBERT EINSTEIN**

In order to understand the all, you have to become the all. If you think you are very wise, a true knower and believe to have understood everything, you are still far from it if you are separate. There cannot be a knower and the thing known as this implies duality. You have to become it or That.

A mind which is beset and divided by choices and confused by alternatives is devoid of power. Ambiguity, indecision and inconstancy create instability of mind and nothing can be accomplished. Single-minded devotion to any cause gives power. The *metanoia* is a conversion of thinking to an expanded awareness of possibilities. The *metanoia* restructures basic representations or models of reality from the past orientation and gives them new life and new meaning. For instance, the concept of a family, in the last hundred years, has undergone a *metanoia*. Farmers had children to work in the fields, a nuclear family developed around a man working and a woman raising children to families with step-children from different marriages. Changes in consciousness can be progressive or regressive.

Because the present world situation is marked by conflict based on disparities between the have and have-nots, a consumer-oriented society which exploits the environment and a dearth of moral values, a human renaissance is needed. The age of partial views, divisive ideas and ideology must be replaced with a view of shared unity. *Metanoia* is a restructuring of a world-view. Morality cannot be legislated so the laws will have to be written in man's heart. The *metanoia* will have to start with individuals before any meaningful rules can be imposed upon society. Evolution is consciousness reflecting back upon itself and learning from its mistakes; not automaton machine-like production with blind machine-like robotic individuals seeking to consume more and return less.

Ancient societies are replete with literature describing wisdom, beauty and psychological insight. The text of ancient India, Egypt, and China are often strange and alien to our modern society and wholly inaccessible to our modern way of thinking. Our Yoga, if you will, is sense-based empirical science employed entirely to technology with the ideal of material domination and the devaluation of the human spirit. Our *metanoia* should be based on the ethic and morality of previous golden ages.

The primary requisite for a great culture is one which builds character. In the earth's chronicles there were periods when societies were built on character development. A great deal of writing by Confucius has dominated China for 2,500 years. Also, his disciples, Chuang Tzu, Ye Tse Tse Chan and Mencius promulgated ethical and moral beliefs. Ironically, wealth was measured by these qualities which cost nothing, while those who possessed great material wealth without the qualities of character building were considered poor indeed.

Lao Tse, who taught *The Way of Life,* was a moral giant who taught the Tao. The way is the same for everyone; that is, if you want to talk with God (see Chapter 20) you have to sever your sensate mind from the seat of consciousness. You cannot know the Tao through the senses or through the sensate mind. The Tao is the point of stillness, where all sense obstructions vanish and the clear light of truth is revealed. At that point you can ask the cosmic intelligence any question and receive an answer, but you must dissolve body awareness or body consciousness.

The *metanoia* will have to be a moving away from sense awareness to mind-knowing. The sensory mind is an awareness of motion, vibration and waves; the cosmic thinking of mind-knowing is in the zero point of stillness (see Chapter 24). This awareness of God's presence existed in other cultures before man fell into carnal sensual thinking. Mankind can only advance when it recognises its own divinity. Because the current society has chosen materialism and sensuality over the quietness and stillness of spirit, it has lost peacefulness and has reaped strife, discord and a restlessness which cannot be satiated through the senses. God-intoxicated men have character and sense-intoxicated men have ignoble character.

> *Unto you that fear my name shall the sun of righteousness arise with healing in his wings.*
> **MALACHI 4-2**

REINCARNATION

Reincarnation has not always been a mystery, but present-day Christianity has made it so. Edgar Cayce, a Christian who was not taught reincarnation, elucidated on this mystery when asked the purpose of reincarnation in one of his trance readings:

> Hence when the entity enters the earth plane (with which we are dealing in the present, and which is to be used for each opportunity that is presented for an activity of the mental and soul forces) it is but a period again and again of the application either of the universal forces, that make for a oneness of activity of the soul; or an activity in what becomes the fruitage thereof as destructive forces, or hardships, or influences that make for the tempering of the soul for its purposes, its activities, its desires throughout its experience.
>
> **EDGAR CAYCE 798-4**

The earth, as well as other realms of activity, serve, therefore, as an environment for the education of the soul who is the real "entity". Since each soul has been given free will, the gain or loss depends on how the soul met its *karma*. Space and time, then, were created for the soul to learn patience. In earlier chapters we learn how, according to Hinduism, the soul covers itself in different sheaths or *kosas*. Only in the dense physical, however, is the soul able to meet all the energies of the universe and attain the full *Brahman* or God-realisation.

Evidently, there must be a spectrum of consciousness which makes consciousness stratified until one attains the supreme reality. This ground is the level Buddha reached which is called the *dharmakaya* or the body of reality. When you die and see the light which comes in the beginning of the first bardo, you have an opportunity for liberation by merging into that light (*dharmakaya*).

Reincarnation is an opportunity to meet the effects to which you were a cause and to learn patience by bearing responsibility for your actions. Those who believe in vicarious atonement and who want only one man to bear the sins of the whole world apparently do not understand how the universe works.

Reincarnation is a return to the field of illusion coloured by past *karmic* perceptions which have to be purified by the expiation of *karma* or entering into right *dharma*. Whatever we meet on our *karmic* path is not only what we have sown but also the way that we perceive it to be. This apparent conundrum of perception confuses and confounds us until we see the clear light of truth. As stated earlier, there are several types of visions according to the type and evolution of the being.

There is the *karmic* vision of ordinary beings; that is, ordinary individuals caught in the web of *maya* and illusion. Next, there is the vision of meditators who are piercing the veil of *maya* and, lastly, the vision of realised beings. The luminous beings do not see with a vision of impurity but behold the world as spontaneously pure and full of perfection. That which we perceive our reality to be is the result of crystallising our experience of inner and outer reality lifetime after lifetime. This fallacious reasoning has led us to the assumption that what we see around us is real. Because of *karma* and negative emotions, we adhere to these obfuscations which deflect and obscure our true nature. Our true nature is *Sat-Chit-Ananda* or existence, consciousness and bliss.

Yet, caught in the web of *maya*, illusion and *samsara*, the ego clutches on the idea of separateness, identity and the dichotomy of me and mine. This conditioning has led to contraction, fear and the threat of mortal extinction. It will thwart any attempt to clear away the miasma and fog surrounding the truth of your being. That truth has always been clear and simple. I AM THAT or *TAT TWAM ASI*. You are one with all that is which is basic to the mysteries. Through mindfulness, meditation, discipline and *sadhana*, you can attain the clarity necessary to cut through the false ego.

Reincarnation ceases when all of the games of the mind, all the tapes have been played out. All *karma* is thought, the mind plays tricks and games and leads us into self-deception. The confused mind is the ego mind: the diamond mind is the Buddha mind-full of clarity and compassion. The Buddha awaits outside of the wheel of *samsara* (death and rebirth) and points away from that wheel. He admonishes us not to get caught up in that wheel and directs us into the clear light of truth.

How is it that some souls get on the path of wisdom while others stay on the path of ignorance life after life. In the *Katha Upanishad* there is a conversation between one called Nachiketas and Death:

> *There is the path of wisdom and the path of ignorance. They are far apart and lead to different ends... Abiding in the midst of ignorance, thinking themselves wise and learned, fools go aimlessly hither and thither like the blind led by the blind. What lies beyond life shines not to those who are childish, or careless, or deluded by wealth.*
>
> **KATHA UPANISHAD**

Do we want to be rich and powerful with a bloated ego or do we want to merge with life and be a part of life? The ego is synonymous with death and rebirth, and life is synonymous with union with spirit. Those who say ego is good have not learned to love. No greater love is to lay down your life. Those who seek to save it will lose it.

Ironically, no soul can attain liberation until it has obtained a human birth. Even the celestial gods and goddesses cannot achieve liberation until they have passed through the human stage. Man is not the body. He is the soul which never dies or undergoes a change. In the *Bhagavad Gita* it says:

> *As a man discards worn out clothes and puts on new ones, likewise, the embodied souls cast off worn out bodies and enter into others which are new.*
>
> **BHAGAVAD GITA**

Liberation is the realisation of the soul's immortality. The cycle of birth and death ceases when this is obtained. One has attained *mukti* or freedom. A *jivamukta* is one who is liberated yet still alive in the body.

There is a Law of Continuity which applies to souls who reincarnate. This law is tied in with the Law of *Karma*. Oftentimes, a soul is not able to complete in one short lifespan its desired objective. If a seeker or spiritual disciple came very close to perfection or liberation and died before the goal was attained, then the last thought that was entertained before death took the soul will determine the time and place of the future birth. In the case of such a soul, he may be born in the house of a realised master. In such a birth this soul will seriously devote himself to meditation. He will want to be alone with the infinite or with those who have attained the infinite. He will strive to reach the transcendental and reach the highest abode. When he dies in that life his *karma* will be expiated and if he returns, it will only be to help other souls do the same.

OUR BIRTH IS BUT A SLEEP AND A FORGETTING.
The Soul that rises with us, our life's Star,
Hath had elsewhere its setting,
And cometh from afar.
Not in entire forgetfulness,
And not in utter nakedness,
But trailing clouds of glory do we come
From God, who is our home.
                    WORDSWORTH (IMITATIONS OF IMMORTALITY)

TRUTH

What is truth? The jesting Pilate asked this question of Jesus and was under the delusion that a thousand answers were possible and none of them would suffice. Partial definitions give only glimpses of truth and all the definitions derived from our sensate mind actually obscure the truth. Perhaps, the closest we can get to truth is from nature. It is often said that the truth is the nature of a thing. What is the true "nature" of a man, a beast or of anything in question; moreover, what is it which gives a thing its nature?

Truth is the genuine nature of a man, thing or substance. When asked if a thing is true or false, does it adhere to its essential nature? Truth is that which is real from the standpoint of the Absolute. The Absolute is the eternal, changeless reality which is universally established through creation. Falsity is present when something assumes the role of a true posture and cannot authenticate that role.

The ego subsumes the role of the real Self. When Jesus said your father was a thief, a liar and a robber (speaking about the devil) he was speaking of the illusory self (mortal ego), which stands in for the real Self. A word from the wise is more efficacious than a lifetime of study. The phrase *Tat Twam Asi* or I am That, when meditated upon, will reveal the truth to you. Lord Krishna told Arjuna that there never was a time when you and all these kings and princes were not. Only the real is immortal. *Tat Twam Asi* (I am That) should be studied. I am the real, the eternal and not the illusory ego.

You are in the light: the light is in you; you are the light. You are one with the father of all things—the truth.

How does one go from the sense-based mortal ego to the *Atma* or real Self? There is a rainbow bridge to higher consciousness called the *antakarana*. Starting from the sense of sight, you assert that seeing is believing. Just as the doubting Thomas, you say that I will not believe unless I see. The question should be asked, are all things as real as they seem when ascertained through the sense of sight, touch, taste, hearing, etc.? Is it the eye which sees? The eyes may be wide open and facing the direction of an object, but if the mind is somewhere else, what is seen? You see only because it is the *atma* which illumines your mind. You love because the *atma* is present. You know and understand because the *atma* is knowledge. Joy or *ananda* is within. As you go from the outer consciousness to the inner, you are building the rainbow bridge.

Poets have always known the wonderful truth:

BY ONE PERVADING SPIRIT
Of tones and numbers all things are controlled,
As sages taught, where faith was found to merit
Initiation in that mystery old.
The heavens, whose aspect makes our minds as still
As they themselves appear to be
Innumerable voices fill
With everlasting harmony.
                    WORDSWORTH (THE POWER OF SOUND)

The higher consciousness has been called by many names: cosmic consciousness, *nirvana*, *samadhi*, etc. The Buddhists speak of *nirvana* and the Hindus talk of the *turiya* state. None of these states is conceptual because they are beyond the relationship of subject and object. Their truth can only be known through direct experience. These states are beyond space, time and causation. What can only be described in these states is that which is consciousness itself.

These states are not attainable within the bounds of normal consciousness. In the consciousness of the One there is no flux and relativity, juxtaposition between this or that or perception of subject and object. Definitions are only given in the realm of time, space and causation.

Though these states remain ineffable, we come to know about them through the effects they leave:

> *By their fruits ye shall know them.*
>
> **JESUS (MATT VII 207)**

In Galatians V 22-3, St. Paul enumerated these fruits: truth, love, joy, peace, long-suffering, etc. Likewise, Asoka, the great Buddhist emperor of India, carved in stone similar fruits: truth, gentleness, purity, peace, joyfulness, etc. Hence, we see no matter how different the path we may be following, they all lead to the same goal: peace, joy, freedom, love, etc.

So, when asked about the truth, the great ones remain mute and refuse to describe the truth. There is the charge, of course, that the Buddha was an atheist; the reason being that he did not believe in a God or the soul, the doctrine of *Annatta* or that we do not have a self. This charge is without foundation and he expressed himself very clearly on this point:

> *There is an unborn, an unoriginate, an unmade, an uncompounded; were there not. O mendicants, there would be no escape from the world of the born, the originated, the made, and the compounded.*
>
> **UDANA, VIII 3**

Buddha did not attempt to define the nature of truth, and he steadfastly declared it to be beyond the nature of our concrete senses and minds.

When one attains the truth, then all thoughts cease; one becomes very silent. There is no power of speech left to describe *Brahman*. Imagine a child when first taken to the ocean and then asked to describe the vastness. The finite cannot describe the infinite.

In the beginning this world was Brahman, *the limitless One—limitless to the east, limitless to the south, limitless to the west, limitless to the north, and above and below, limitless in every direction. Truly for him east and other directions exist not, nor across, nor below nor above.*

Incomprehensible is that supreme soul, unlimited, unborn, not to be reasoned about, unthinkable— He whose soul is space. In the dissolution of the world He alone remains awake. From that space He, assuredly, awakes this world, which is a mass of thought by Him, and in Him it disappears.

His is that shining form which gives heat in yonder sun and which is the brilliant light in a smokeless fire, as also the fire in the stomach which cooks the food. For thus has it been said: 'He who is in the fire, and he who is here in the heart, and he who is yonder in the sun—he is the one.'

MAITRI UPANISHAD

The truth cannot be known while you are dreaming. You have to wake up. The truth cannot be known through your five senses. Mirages and holograms appear real and that is the nature of *maya*, of mistaking a rope for a snake. Truth can only be known in the pure light of consciousness, unsullied by carnal senses, egoism, pride, lust, envy, greed, etc. This is why all religions stress discipline, purity and renunciation of the worldly.

Truth cannot be known as an object of study. This is the deepest mystery. The knower (Self) cannot be known for to know itself it would be reduced to an object. Since who you really are is beyond duality you cannot make yourself an object. Hence, we have a paradox, a dilemma if you will, whereby, that which knows all (Self) cannot know itself. This is why the sages remain mute when asked about the ultimate truth.

For thinkers and scientists this is all absurd. They say that there is no Self and that man is just a mechanism, a machine and that consciousness is just an effect of biochemicals, etc. Science itself comes from the Latin *sciere*, meaning to know. They want to know and define the truth. To them, the truth cannot be unknowable, they just need time to find the truth. They have to understand a dimension where the truth cannot be reduced to an object.

> *I am the way, the truth and the life.*
>
> **JESUS**

I am *Sathya* or truth. *Sat* or truth is existence or beingness; therefore, beingness is the truth.

I AM BRAHMAN

Since existence is truth and the root or foundation of the universe, then when we remove the veils of ignorance (ego) we can then know and be one with *Brahman*. The *Atman* is one with *Brahman* which forms the basis for the statement I Am That. The terms *Brahman* and *Atman* refer to "that" and "thou" respectively. Because there is no difference between the Self and God, then duality disappears and I Am or existence remains as an undivided whole.

Brahman is a term often used to describe God, the Ruler of the universe, and *Atman* is the individual soul. When the individual soul realises his identity with *Brahman*, then the soul can say I am *Brahman* or I am God. The Self or God is reality. Soul is its reflection. When the soul, which has been given free will, assigns its will entirely to the will of God, there is no more individual free will; then, all that it does is the reflection of the will of God. This is what Jesus meant when he said, "I only do what the Father does."

We are all puppets and are under the play of *maya*. God is the master puppeteer:

> *Arjuna, the Lord dwells in the hearts of all beings, who are mounted on the automation of this body, causing them by His illusive power to revolve (according to their actions).*
> **BHAGAVAD GITA (CHAPTER XVIII, VERSE 61)**

Soul is given being by being a reflection of That or the
Self. The soul is being. The Self is neither being nor non-
being. The Self is attribute-less yet has hands and feet
everywhere; eyes, head, face everywhere; ears everywhere.
Though it is the perceiver of all sense objects, it lacks all
senses. Though it lacks all senses, it is the sustainer and
enjoyer of all qualities of nature. The soul, being a reflection
of the Self, is feminine, whereas the Self is masculine, hence,
the references in the *Bible* to the bride and the bridegroom.

Now if *Brahman* is the only reality, then how does the
individual soul fit in that reality? *Brahman* and *Atma* are
identical and it is the world which is illusory due to the
creation of *maya* within the realm of manifestation. Outside
the realm of manifestation He transcends definition and
cannot be defined as one or as many. Thus, the *Upanishads*
say that He is the limited and the limitless, the One without a
second and that whatever is perceived is Him. The manifest
world is the play of His consciousness in its infinite aspect and
is, thus, real. Everything and all is God.

Each embodied soul with its seeming separate and
individual nature is God. This *Brahman* cannot be expressed
in words or understood by the mind. It is both personal and
impersonal. He is the creator, preserver and destroyer of the
universe—Vishnu, Shiva and Brahma. Only by the removal of
ignorance *(avidya)* can *Brahman* be understood.

The *Atman* assumes the so-called limitations or the
coatings of the intellect, because it mistakenly thinks itself to
be this coating, which is totally different from itself. The man
who is in fact this *Atman* takes himself to be separate from it,
and from *Brahman*, who is the one *Atman* in all creatures.
Likewise, an ignorant person may perceive a pot different
from the clay which it is made from.

Now, what is written in the *Upanishads* is the very
highest idea that the Self and *Brahman* are one. This
removes the veils of mystery between God and man. In truth,
we are not the separate, individual waves of consciousness,
apart from the ocean of cosmic consciousness, but are in

reality the ocean of consciousness as the waves. That we are
a wave is ignorance, *avidya* or nescience. God has become
man who is the ocean of consciousness.

I think not 'I know well';
Yet I know not 'I know not'!
He of us who knows it, knows it;
Yet he knows not 'I know not.'

It is conceived of by him by whom it is not
    conceived of.
He by whom It is conceived of, knows It not.
It is not understood by those who [say they]
    understand It.
It is understood by those who [say they] understand
    It not.

                                    KENA UPANISHAD

Unless man knows that he is *Brahman* (God) then no real
transformation of the earth is possible. This knowledge,
though ancient, of man's nature being identical to God, is a
necessary stage for humanity to attain before an enduring
civilisation of unity and brotherhood can be established. The
mysteries or secrets of the universe cannot be found in the
visible universe. It can only be found in the invisible universe
which creates and controls the visible. It is now time for
humanity to know God as He is. All of man's erroneous and
fallacious understanding of the universe has come through his
outer vision of the senses and not upon his inner mind-
knowing. We see illusion through our senses which the
ancients called *maya*. Mind-knowing is God-knowing. When
Jesus said, "I and my father are one," he was saying his mind
and God's mind were one. The centring invisible energy is
God's mind and your mind. You cannot see it but you know it.

I am *Brahman*. I am God. I am light. I am love. I am law.
Atma Vidya or knowledge of one's *Atma* is *Brahma vidya* or
knowledge of God. In the undivided, unobstructed, sexless,

unconditioned universe, God is invisible, unmoving white magnetic light of the all-powerful, all-knowing and ever-present mind. When God knows, He is magnetic; when He thinks, He is electric. His universe of magnetic light is always at rest and is balance. His electric universe, likewise, must be balanced by action and reaction.

God is the one still magnetic light at the centre which divides His omnipresence by extending two poles. God, the knower (as father and mother) divides His sexlessness to extend sexed-pole father and mother from His Oneness. The only desire of these divided pairs is to unite to void their separateness. This is how the electric universe is formed. In cause, God is One; in effect He is three. Just as in the Trinity, the One God subsumes the other two. Man's mind and God's mind are one. I am *Brahman*. Man, like God, decentrates his thinking to form an idea, and concentrates to create a body in the image of his idea. Life is motion in the electric universe and death is the rest of the still magnetic universe. The magnetic life is eternal life and life in physical body is but a pulsing simulation of God's eternal life in the one God.

At last your question of who am I is answered. Who you are is *Brahman*. You are no different from Him. You are not the body. You are not the organs of perception. You are not the vital forces nor even the thinking mind. Nor are you the unconscious mind or the mind's latent tendencies. You are pure awareness or *Sat-Chit-Ananda* or existence-consciousness and bliss.

THE ANCIENT NARROW PATH THAT STRETCHES FAR AWAY
Has been touched by me, has been found by me.
Be it the wise, the knowers of Brahman, *go up*
Hence to the heavenly world, released.

BRIHADARANYAKA UPANISHAD

LIFE

You cannot forever remain in the abyss of unknowing. Life has a way of finding the answers and seeking broader avenues of expression. Jesus was a revolutionary. The Pharisaical orders, habits, dogmas and ways of the world could not hold him. He told us that we could break free also. Crystallised dogmas are not greater than life and cannot hold the current of the abundant life to come. It seems like he denounced religious dogma by calling them liars, thieves and evil. How then did all the dogma get reinstated after a period of time on earth? Life is not in religion or dogma and never will be.

Beware you scribes and pharisees, you hypocrites who block progress from people; you will not attain it easily and you keep it from those who wish to attain it because of false teachings.

JESUS OF NAZARETH

It is too bad that much human blood was shed in the name of this teacher who did not set out to teach that He was greater than us but to show that man is divine and not just a singular individual. The God within him and you is the same Omnipresent God where life comes from.

Each of us has the "I am God" or "I am Brahman" within us and the life which belonged to him also belongs to you. Man becomes the victim of illusions and is forever searching. The problem is man cannot find the truth in the sensory world and has to go within like all the other great teachers did. He cannot have Jesus, Buddha or Lao Tse do it for him. Just as man cannot have another take on his sins. There is a difference in thinking and knowing. Just as Jesus said, the outer mortal man can do nothing; however, the inner, knowing living soul can. These teachers taught us our next stage of development, but we have to do it ourselves. We have to find this inner dynamic knowledge and identity of the presence of God within our own souls and throughout nature. Then we will have more abundant life.

The reason we haven't yet found God ourselves is because of our infancy and barbarous practices of pagan religious beliefs. We must know the mysteries of life and death and how we still retain our identity after death. We must go beyond the illusory realm of mere physical appearances. Mind has to pierce the illusion of the senses. What we know about the world is not what the illumined ones know. They know from the inner realm of cause and not the outer of effect.

As stated in earlier chapters, the two forces—centripetal and centrifugal—form the yin and yang of the complete Tao. Life and death are just opposing opposites of a cycle. There are two forms in the universe which represent this cycle, the sphere and the cube. The male centripetal forces condense to form incandescent suns and the female centrifugal forces expand to the cold cube of space. Compression and expansion take place ceaselessly in this spirallic wave universe, and it is the white magnetic light which centres them both.

Living bodies are made by the centripetal force of compression. Dying bodies find their release by expansion. The centrifugal force is a desire to return to the zero universe of rest and unwinds that which has been compressed out of it.

Wherever motion is, it is centred by stillness and from that stillness is cause. Life springs from cause and not from effects. The still magnetic light is cause. God creates in the same way we do from a centre of stillness. "Be still and know that *I am God.*"

The two opposite conditions of pressure which control all life-death cycles are: the positive condition of compression which pulls inward toward a centring zero of rest to form the result of compression-gravity and the negative condition of expansion which outwardly thrusts and radially expands from a centring zero of rest to form a low potential of space. That which we call the life-death cycle is the cubed sphere. The compressed condition of the universe is exactly equal to the expanded condition. Suns die and explode radially and the black cold space condenses to form suns. The universe is a giant pump of expansion and compression.

As you concentrate and decentrate your thinking idea, you create a life and death cycle of your own in the electric wave universe; yet, in the still white light of the magnetic universe of cause there is no life-death cycle going on.

> *The Self, which is free from evil, ageless, deathless, sorrowless, hungerless, thirstless, whose desire is the Real, whose conception is the Real—He should be searched out, Him one should desire to understand. He obtains all worlds and all desires who has found out and who understands that Self.*
> CHANDOGYA UPANISHAD

Unless you know yourself to be the pure essence or the pure Self, you do not know what life really is. All names and forms which go to make up this universe and constitute its nature are creations of the mind. The mind, therefore, has to be controlled and its waywardness calmed. Once the mind is self-controlled, you will gradually get to know your true Self. You must learn to meditate on your *Atma*-hood and learn to see the universal in the particular.

You can learn to see without eyes, hear without ears, and speak without a tongue, smell without a nose, feel or touch without a body, and walk without legs. Finally, experience without even the mind. You are, after all, the pure undefiled essence itself; you are the Supreme Self.

Finally, all mysteries—ancient and modern—will be revealed and the play of *maya* will be discovered as a play and then you will have the sure conviction that you are God and God is you. Remember this basic *Brahman* in the universe:

> *I will keep him in perfect peace whose mind is stayed on me.*
>
> Isaiah

You have to be ever vigilant. The senses might recoil upon you at any moment, especially when you are out in the world. The basic truth must be kept constantly before your mind. "I am Brahman." Once you know *Brahman* you become *Brahman*. The fact that this world is unreal (*maya*) and *Brahman* is real must become patently obvious to you. The *mahatmas* or great souls who have won this realisation deserve your worship. You worship them as they worship the God within you. This is the great mystery of all the scriptures: the *Vedas*, the *Upanishads*, the *Bible*, the *Koran*, the *Book of Dyzan* and the *Shastras*. Life is only worthwhile when this mystery is solved.

Truth and untruth have to be cut apart with a razor-sharp sword of wisdom. Life is not meant to be lived in ignorance. This ignorance which delays and denies the inquiry into the nature of *atman* makes delusion and *maya* propagate. *Brahman* alone is, was and will continue to be. Know this, know the truth and then you can truly live.

We come to know God by an Incarnation of God: Krishna speaks—

> *I AM THE BIRTHLESS, THE DEATHLESS,*
> *Lord of all that breathes..*
> *I seem to be born;*
> *It is only seeming,*
> *Only my maya.*
> *I am still master of my Prakriti,*
> *The power that makes me.*
> *He who knows the nature*
> *Of my task and my holy birth*
> *Is not reborn*
> *When he leaves this body,*
> *He comes to me.*
>
> **LORD KRISHNA**

Likewise, compare the above lines with the words of the *Bible:*

> *But as many as received him, to them gave he power to become the sons of God; even to them that believe in his name.*
>
> **JOHN I. 12**

To know an Incarnation of God is to know God. To see the invisible God one must look at the divine incarnations. To worship a Buddha, a Krishna or a Jesus, however, is not to worship a man as God or worship a person; you must worship the impersonal/personal existence of man/God and God/man. These divine incarnations are the doorways to life and give us the keys to unlock greater life.

CONCLUSION

There will always be mysteries as long as there is mind to play games. As long as we play hide and seek with our true nature, mysteries will abide. The greatest mystery is ourself. We do not yet recognise our divinity. Teachers have come and instructed us, but we somehow think it is still out there. There is no out there. The world does not exist, except as a play of *maya*. *Maya* is real like a dream is real. When you awake, the dream is gone.

Even the planets, sun, moon, earth, etc., are all inside you. The outside does not exist except as a projection. You not only have planets, but universes inside you as well; they are called *chakras*. Since you are God, there are also so many beings who live inside you.

We give a name and a form to understand God in illusion (*maya*); however, if a person says that a certain form of God is the only God, then that person is in an illusion within an illusion. Whatever we have to learn is already inside of us; we cannot get it from the outside by any means. You can have many teachers or gurus, but at last there is only one—your Self. The one who knows his true Self does not need a teacher or a guru.

Basically, your greatest desire is your world. The universe can play all kinds of games with you. You and everyone else have their own model or paradigm to play with. Each person's universe is different according to the preponderance of his desires. It is because of these desires that we are all caught in the web of *maya*.

This book mainly focuses on the male and female aspects of creation; such as, the centripetal and centrifugal forces in the universe. Because we live in the world of duality it is these dual forces of yin and yang and their interplay which has created all of this. As Lao Tse describes the Tao of yin and yang, these two furies produced the ten thousand things. In Hinduism it is the One which has become many.

In the West, we speak of evolution in terms of science, biology and nature which pertain only to the form side of life. In Hinduism, *Pravriti* is the stage of evolution where the creative energy is flowing downward. The opposite of *Pravriti* is *Nivriti* or involution, the stage of evolution where energy is drawn inward and upward toward the realisation of the Self. Looking at *Pravriti* as a triangle pointing downward and *Nivriti* as a triangle pointing upward, one can recognise the Star of David which is the balance between these two forces. In the East, *yantras* are also used as models to describe how energy works in the universe. No matter what model is used to explain cosmic mysteries, they all have to be experienced first-hand. Then, like the parable of the cave, a mystery revealed cannot be easily explained. The main purpose of this book is to ask questions and then go beyond rhetorical questions to true seeking: Start by asking Who Am I? By this inquiry, you will reach the Self.

True seeking is looking behind and beyond appearances. Sai Baba materialises sacred ash called *vibhuti*. This ash is a potent reminder that everything in the material world is reduced to ash and then no further reduction is possible. Our houses, our clothing, our money, the trees, grass, etc., when burnt, are all reduced to ashes. Likewise, our desires, the body, the senses, when on fire by the knowledge of *Brahman*, become *Brahman*. Hence, a knower of *Brahman* lives in freedom from body consciousness.

A knower of *Brahman* is in the body but is not of the body. He sees the body as a shadow of his true Self. If a man does identify himself as the body, then he will experience pleasure and pain, good and evil; however, he who has realised the *Atman*, such fetters have fallen from him. *Atma-Vidya* is *Brahma-Vidya*. He is not exalted when people praise him nor is he debased when people criticise him. He is beyond the pairs of opposites. He walks alone and is desireless amidst desire. He is vigilant and sees the *Atman* in all things. Rich or poor, he is unattached. He may appear mad, childish, wise, foolish or whatever. He is always free to wander the earth seeing only freedom in the *Atman*.

The mystery, both ancient and modern, is our own true Self.

GLOSSARY OF TERMS

Abba: Father

Advaita Vedanta: Philosophy of non-dualism.

Ahamkara: The ego or separated self which takes itself to be the real Self.

Ahimsa: Non-violence.

Ahriman: The anti-Christ.

Ahura Mazda: Zoroastrianism—the solar logos.

Ajna: The sixth *chakra* or third eye.

Ananda: Bliss

Ananda-maya-kosa: One of the five sheaths or coverings of the soul.

Annatta: Doctrine of no-self as taught by Buddha.

Annus Magnus: A great year in astrology, approximately 26,000 years.

Anu: The ultimate physical atom.

Antakarana: Rainbow bridge to higher consciousness.

Arhat: In Buddhism, one who has reached soul awareness.

Arjuna: The third among the Pandavas, to whom Lord Sri Krishna taught the Bhagavad Gita.

Asoka: Buddhist emperor in ancient India.

Astral Body: The subtle body which is a prototype of the gross physical body.

Asurya: Demons who shun the light.

Atma: The individual soul which is a part of God.

Atma-Vichara: Self-inquiry or "Who am I?"

Atma-vidya: Knowledge of one's soul or *atma*.

Aum: Monosyllabic, mystical sound symbol of God. It is the word *(pranava)* that was God and represents the Trinity, the three stages of consciousness, the three worlds, the three bodies and beyond.

Avatara: Descent of God or divine beings.

Avidya: Ignorance or nescience.

Avyakta: The imperceptible, homogeneous substance that is called *prakriti*.

Axis Mundi: Pole of the world.

Azoth: Refined spiritual essence.

Baba: Father

Bhagavad Gita: Bible of India. Song of God. The teachings of Lord Krishna to Arjuna which contain the essence of the *Vedas*.

Bhakti: Devotion and love for the Lord.

Bharat: Ancient name for India: translates as Lovers of the Lord.

Bindu: A dot or point of manifestation.

Bodhisattva: Buddhism. One who completes his evolution on earth but who chooses to return for the upliftment of humanity.

Brahma: One of the gods in Hindu Trinity: Brahma creates, increases.

Brahma-jnana: One who possesses knowledge of *Brahman*.

Brahmachari: A celibate student of the Veda under the spiritual supervision of a mentor.

Brahman: The impersonal, featureless, unmanifested principle that is the Godhead. The origin and cause of the universe whose characteristics are: absolute existence *(Sat)*, absolute consciousness *(chit)* and absolute bliss *(ananda)*.

Brahman Randhra: Seventh *chakra*.

Brahma-vidya: Knowledge of God.

Buddhi: Intelligence. That faculty which enables the mind to perceive objects in the phenomenal world.

Chakras: Spiritual centres of consciousness.
Chela: Student.
Chi: Cosmic energy.
Chit: Consciousness; wisdom.
Chitta: Mind stuff. The mental mode turned toward objects.
   That aspect of the mind in which impressions are stored.

Darshan: Vision or sight of a holy being.
Deva: A god or celestial being. A "shining one". Angel.
Devi: Mother goddess.
Dharma: Virtuous deeds; harmonious life; a person's natural
   duty. Also, may be construed as inherent qualities. This is
   also the law of God which sustains and upholds society
   and the universe.
Dharmakaya: Body of light. The ground for the luminous
   Self.
Dhyana: Meditation on the lighted flame *(jyoti)*.
Dwarpara Yuga: The third of the four cycles into which time
   is divided by the Hindus. The Copper Age.
Gayatri: Oldest prayer in the world.
Ghana: Path of wisdom.
Granthi Knot: Nexus of ego.
Grihastha: Householder.
Gunas: The three modes of nature. The three fundamental
   qualities, tendencies, or stresses which underlie all
   manifestation; *sattva, rajas,* and *tamas,* characterised as
   white, red, and black, respectively.
Guru: Spiritual teacher or preceptor. One who can bring you
   from darkness to light.

Indriyas: Senses
Isha: The Supreme Lord. A form of Sai.
Ishtadevta: Favourite form or personality of the Lord, Jesus,
   Krishna, Sai Baba, etc.
Ishwara (Ishvara): The name of the Supreme Lord indicating
   his lordship of the worlds.
Jagath: The world as outpictured by the mind.

Jiva: The individual soul or ego.

Jivamukta: One who has realised the supreme identity while still alive in the body.

Jnana: Knowledge of the absolute transcending form and formlessness.

Jnana-Marga: Path of wisdom.

Jnana maya kosa: Wisdom sheath.

Jyoti: Spiritual light.

Kalchakra: Wheel of time.

Kali-Yuga: Age of darkness. Iron Age. The present historical age, fourth and last in a perpetually repeating cycle of four progressively degenerate ages.

Kosa: Sheath or covering of the soul.

Kama: Lust or desire.

Karma: Action and reaction.

Karma-yoga: Path of spiritual elevation through selfless, non-fruitive actions dedicated to the Supreme.

Kroda: Anger

Kundalini: The yogic principle of serpent power. The primal *maya*.

Lao Tse: Chinese philosopher who taught the Way of Life—Taoism.

Leela: Divine sport.

Lobda: Greed.

Mahabharata: The great epic history of ancient India.

Mahat: The intellectual principle.

Mahatma: Great soul.

Mahimas: Powers.

Manas: The mind, understanding (man to think), thinking faculty.

Manna: Energy in Huna science.

Mantra: Incantation, hymn. Constant repetition produces results.

Maya: Illusion. False appearance.
Mana maya kosa: Mental sheath.
Metanoia: Restructuring of the mind.
Monad: The one individual being.
Mudra: Hand postures, part of worship.
Mukta: A liberated person.
Mukti: Liberation.

Nirguna Brahman: World of uncreated or formless world.
Nirvana: Bliss sheath.
Nirvakalpa samadhi: Mergence into the One with no subject/object differentiation. The highest state of concentration, in which the soul loses all sense of separation from the Universal Self, but a temporary state from which there is a return to ego or body consciousness.
Nivriti: Liberation from worldly existence, renunciation.
Nouemenal: Opposite of phenomenal. World of nous or divine ideas.
Nous: Divine sphere (Platonic).

Ouranos: Greek for heaven.

Paramatma: The Supreme Self.
Paramahamsa: One who has merged into the supreme swan *(hamsa),* or God.
Prakriti: Nature.
Pralaya: Inbreathing of the cosmic breath.
Prana: Vital energy.
Prarabdha Karma: Fructifying action or ripe *karma.*
Prasad: Food that is blessed.
Prashanthi Nilayam: Abode of the highest peace. Sai Baba's *ashram.*
Pravriti: Stage of evolution.
Prema: Love.
Premaswarupa: Embodiment of love.

Prima Materia: Baseness of matter.
Puranas: The 18-epic text expounding the teachings of the Vedas.
Purusha: (literally, "the enjoyer")
1. The Supreme enjoyer (of *prakriti*, nature).
2. The individual *jiva* (living being), enjoyer of the physical body.

Rajas: Continued activity, predilection toward worldly life. One of the three *gunas*. Activity.

Sadhaka: Disciple.
Sadhana: A path toward liberation.
Sadhu: Ascetic.
Saguna Brahman: God with form.
Sahaj samadhi: Unbroken *samadhi* in which all levels of creation are a part of consciousness.
Samadhi: Superconsciousness.
Samsara: Wheel of death and rebirth.
Samskaras: Impressions or residue from past lives.
Sanathana Dharma: The ancient highway to God.
Sankalpa: Will, volition, mental activity, thought, tendencies.
Sannyasin: One who has renounced the world.
Sannyasa: Renunciation.
Sat: Pure existence; pure being.
Sat Purush: God as the indweller in the heart.
Sat-Chit-Ananda: Existence, consciousness, bliss.
Sathya: Truth.
Sathya Graha: The force of truth.
Sathya Yuga: Golden Age or Age of Truth.
Sathya Sai Baba: Avatar living in S. India.
Sattva: Purity; one of the three *gunas*.
Savikalpa Samadhi: Samadhi distinguished by retention of subject and object.
Self: God.

Shakti: The manifesting energy of a divine aspect; represented mythologically as the wife of God/Divine Mother.

Shamballa: Etheric retreat in the Gobi Desert.

Shema: Hebrew for "listen". Describes the One God.

Shetra: Field of life.

Shiva: God of destruction.

Sutratma: Thread of energy from the divine monad to the personality beating down on the fontanelle.

Sukshmabuthas: Subtle electricity.

Tamas: Darkness, ignorance; involution, one of the three *gunas*.

Tao: Philosophy of Lao Tse. Yin and yang.

Taoism: Chinese philosophy.

Tapas: Austerities.

Tat: Brahman; That.

Tat-Twam-Asi: "That thou Art."

Turiya: The fourth state or witness consciousness; everpresent and unchanging as against states of waking, dreaming and deep sleep. Highest *samadhi* where you become one with *Brahman*.

Upanishads: Philosophical writings forming part of the *Vedas*. It literally means at "the knee of listening" or "to sit close". These doctrines were so named because these secrets and mysteries were personally imparted to the disciple by the teacher.

Vairagya: Detachment from the world; renunciation.

Vajra: Tibetan Buddhism; the diamond sceptre. Shows union of opposites.

Vasanas: Subtlest form of desire which remains in the causal body.

Vedas: Revealed knowledge as embodied in the four holy books of the Hindus, which are called *Rig Veda, Yajur*

Veda and *Atharva Veda,* as revealed through *Rishis* or holy men.

Vichara: Enquiry into the truth of the Self.

Vibhuti: Sacred ash materialised by Sai Baba.

Vishnu: God as preserver. One of the Hindu Trinity.

Vishwarupa: Cosmic form of the Lord.

Vivarta: The on-rolling process in which the One God becomes many.

Yantra: Geometric designs.

Yoga: A system of spiritual discipline for approaching the Supreme.

Yogi: One who practises a system of yoga.

Yoga Bhastra: One who has fallen from the path.

Zen: Introduced in China in the 6th century and Japan in the 12th century. Emphasis on enlightenment by direct intuitive perception.

Zoroastrian: One who follows the Persian religion and its founder Zoroaster.